GILLOW
FURNITURE
DESIGNS

GILLOW
FURNITURE
DESIGNS

1760–1800

Edited and introduced by

LINDSAY BOYNTON

The Bloomfield Press
1995

Published by The Bloomfield Press, P.O. Box 8, Royston, Herts
SG8 8TA, United Kingdom.
Copyright © 1995 by Lindsay Boynton
All rights reserved. This book may not be reproduced, in whole
or in part, in any form (beyond that copying permitted by
Sections 107 and 108 of the U.S. Copyright Law and except
by reviewers for the public press), without written permission
from the publisher.

Designed by Jeffrey Sains
Set in Linotron Bembo and printed in Hong Kong through World Print Ltd.

ISBN 0 9525115 09

CONTENTS

ACKNOWLEDGEMENT

Grateful thanks are due to the Isobel Thornley Bequest (University of London) for a grant in aid of the publication of this book.

This book is published with the assistance of a loan from the Marc Fitch Fund, to which grateful acknowledgement is made.

FOREWORD

During my Gillow research as a whole I have incurred an enormous debt of gratitude which I look forward to acknowledging in my forthcoming book on *Gillow Furniture*. Here my obligations are easier to mention. First, I am most grateful to Miss Margaret Swarbrick, Chief Archivist of the Westminster City Archives, for facilitating my work and in particular for allowing reproduction of the designs; also to her colleagues who for years patiently got out and put away each day my ever-growing collection of record-card boxes. Second, it is a pleasure to thank Peter Hirst-Smith, who has photographed Gillow items for me over many years, for the illustrations which were mostly taken by him. The photographs of the clock cases were kindly loaned by Sir Nicholas Goodison.

I have long wished to publish an edition of selected Gillow designs, both as a milestone towards my monograph on Gillows and because of their intrinsic importance. This book was to have been published commercially but it fell victim to the recession. The subscription method adopted as an alternative attracted an encouraging level of support, and I am grateful to all those who were prepared to subscribe in advance: their names are recorded below. However, publication would not have been possible without a generous subsidy from the sponsors who contributed to an appeal fund organized by Christopher Gilbert, Andrew Jenkins, and Martin Levy: I thank them all most warmly.

L.B.

LIST OF SPONSORS

Norman Adams Limited
Anonymous
Apter Fredericks Ltd.
Avon Antiques
G.A. Baines
H.C. Baxter & Sons
H. Blairman & Sons
Arthur Brett & Sons Ltd.
The British Antique Dealers' Association
Charles Cator
Graham Child
Richard Courtney Ltd.
Dreweatt Neate
The Oliver Ford Trust
C. Fredericks & Son Ltd.
J.D. Friedman
Jonathan Harris
W.R. Harvey & Co (Antiques) Ltd.
Haughey Antiques
J.B. Hawkins Antiques
Hotspur Ltd.
John Hyman and Betty Leviner
Jeremy Ltd.
John Keil Ltd.
Peter Lang
Lawrence Fine Art Auctioneers
David Love
Charles Lumb & Sons Ltd.
James McWhirter
Florian Papp Inc.
Pelham Galleries Ltd.
Phillips of Hitchin (Antiques) Ltd.
Ronald Phillips Ltd.
Caroline Rimell
Larry J. Sirolli
Sotheby's
Stair & Co Ltd.
M. Turpin Ltd.
Charles Walford
Patrick Walker
Graham Watson
John A. Werwaiss
Windsor House Antiques (Leeds) Ltd.
Woolley & Wallis

LIST OF SUBSCRIBERS

Canon E.M. Abbott
Robert Adam
Norman Adams Ltd.
Mr. Martin Ainscough
Mr. Peter John Ainsworth
C. Aldred
Juan Pelaez y Fabra, Marques de Alella
Mr. N.J. Alexander
Dr. Brian Allen
Rosamond Allwood
Bibliotheek Rijksmuseum, Amsterdam
Philip Andrade
Stephen Anson, Esq.
Apter-Fredericks Ltd.
Mr. J. Arnold
I.V. Askew
Asprey
Avon Antiques

Mrs. Daphne Baker
Sir Richard Baker Wilbraham, Bt.
Mr. G.A. Baines
William Baldry-Vincent
Simon Baldwick
Ms. A. Bambery (Pickfords House
    Museum, Derby)
W.L. Banks
Dr. T.C. Barnard
R.M. Barockh Antiques, Los Angeles
Mr. J.P. Bartlam
Francis Baxendale
H.C. Baxter & Sons
Dr. Geoffrey Beard
Canon John Douglas Beckwith
William Bedford Plc.
Mr. John R. Bernasconi
Laurance Black Ltd.
H. Blairman & Sons Ltd.
Boardman Fine Art Auctioneers
Mr. A.F. Boddy
J.R.E. Borron, Esq.
Adam Bowett
Miss Sarah Bowles
Mr. E.G.L. Boyd
Mr. Robert Bradley
Arthur Brett & Sons Ltd.
Central Library, Bristol
Department of Medieval and Later
    Antiquities, The British Museum
Mr. C.J. Brittain
L.G. Brown

Mrs. L. Mary Brown
Mrs. Pamela Rose Brown
Peter B. Brown, Esq.
Mr. A. Brownsword
P. Anthony Bull
Edward Bulmer Esq.
Angela Burgin
R.M. Burton, Esquire
The Business & Medical Centre Ltd.
Mr. Roderick Butler
Robin Butler
Adrian Butterworth
David Richmond Byers III
H.N.D. Byway

Caledonian Inc., Winnetka, Illinois
The Lord Camoys
Mr. R.P. Cannell
Mr. Roger Carling
Mr. Matthew Carrington
David Carstairs
Mr. & Mrs. G.F. Carter
Simon Cass
Charles Cator
R.C. Cave & Sons Ltd.
Cavendish Fine Arts
B.E. Chapman Esq.
Mr. M. Chapman
Graham Child
Christie's
J.F. Cipkin
Richard E. Cleverdon
John Coleman
Anthony Coleridge
Collins Antiques
Colonial Williamsburg Foundation
Martyn Cook Antiques Pty Ltd.,
    Woollahra, NSW
Mr. Paul O. Cooke
Alex Copland
Robert Copley, Esq.
John Cornforth
Thomas Coulborn & Sons
Mrs. T.A. Coultas
The Country Seat
Paul Couts Ltd.
Prof. A.D. Cox
Mr. Tom Craig
Mr. J.A. Cropper
Mr. John M. Cross
M.D. Cruickshanks, Esq.

Mr. Jonathan Cull
Nelli Q. Curti
Mr. Eldred Christian Curwen

Mr. Philip Dalziel
Sir Francis Dashwood, Bt.
Mrs. Jane Davies
Dawson U.K. Ltd.
Keith Dawson
Mr. Kenneth Dibben
Dingwall and Banks
Dorking Desk Shop
Mr. Philip J. Doyle
Martin Dru Drury, Esq.
Mr. M.J. Durkee
Mr. John Duxfield

Richard Eaton
John Ebdon
B.E. Elridge
E. Elliott
Mr. Giles Ellwood
R. Eldridge
Mr. R.R. Emanuel
English Heritage, Kenwood
David W. Evans, B.A. (Hons), M. Soc. Sc.
Mrs. S.C.S. Farmer
Sir Matthew Farrer, KCVO
James Feisenberger
Alan G. Fenton
Mr. Mark Fitzgerald
G.W. Ford & Son Ltd.
The Rev. Wilbert Forker
G.H.C. & R. Freeman

Stephen Timothy Dryden Garland
Major W.F. Garnett
Mr. C.G. Gilbert
Mrs. Catharine Gill
Bernadette Gillow
Mr. Charles H.P. Gillow
J.T. Gillow
Mr. W.P. Gillow
R.H. Glossop
Gallery Antiques Limited
Dr. R.B. Godwin-Austen
Sir Nicholas Goodison
Alan Gore
Mr. Edgar A. Grantham
Mr. L.R. Greenough
Miss Silvia D. Greenwood
Anthony Gregg
Mr. H. Gregory
John D. Griffin, Esq.

Paul D. Grinke
The Hon. Julian Guest

David Hales
Richard Halford
Dr. Ivan Hall
Mr. G. Hamilton
G.C. Hancock
Jonathan Harris
P.A. Harrison
Andrew Hartley Fine Arts
W.R. Harvey & Co. Ltd.
R. Hasell-McCosh, Esq.
Haughey Antiques
Mr. John Hawkins
Mrs. Helena Hayward
J.G.S. Hayward, Esq.
Mr. Algernon Heber-Percy
Mrs. A.C. Heseltine
Philip Hewat-Jaboor
Heytesbury Antiques
Mrs. Hibbert-Foy
Carlton Hobbs Ltd.
Mr. Peter J. Holmes
Mr. Giles Hopkinson
Hotspur Ltd.
Hirsch Library, The Museum of Fine Arts, Houston
Mr. Julian Howard
The Hon. Simon Howard
Mr. H.J. Hyams
John A. Hyman/Betty C. Leviner

Ivor Ingall
Brand Inglis
Gervase Jackson-Stops, Esq.
Anthony James & Son Ltd.
L.S.A. Jarrett
Patrick Jefferson
Jeremy Ltd.
Simon Jervis F.S.A.
Michael M.O. Jodrell
Peter J.W. Johnson
Mr. Paul Johnston
K.H. Jones
Mr. Philip Jones
R. Jones
C. Jussel

Mr. J. Kaner
Mr. J.D.M. Karczewski-Slowikowski
Mr. B. Kearsley
John Keil Limited
Miss Alison Kelly
Timothy Kendrew

Ms. Sara Kenny
Piers Kettlewell
Anthony Kilroy
Mr. Robert Kime
Ian J. King
Mr. D.J.M. Kitson
Trevor H. Kyle, A.I.A. (Scot.)

Lancashire County Library
Peter Lang, New York
Claire Langley
Neil Lanham
Lauder & Howard
Mr. Robert J. Lawford
Lawrence Fine Art Ltd.
Terence R. Leach
D.M. Learmont
Charles B. Lee
Leeds City Art Galleries
Michael Legg
Lennox Money Antiques Ltd.
Mr. David Letham
Mr. R.F. Lindley
Mr. Julian Carr Linford
David H.B. Litt
Mr. Robin W. Little
Mrs. Kay Livesey
Mr. Esme C.H. Lowe
Mr. David Love
Charles Lumb & Sons Ltd.
Frank and Barbara Lupton
Mr. John McClenaghan
Cameron McEachern Organisation Pty
  Limited
Mr. A.M. McGreevy
Mr. A.M. Mackay
Maggie McKean
K.J.C. Macmaster
Paul Maitland-Smith
Felicity Mallet
The Manchester Metropolitan University
  Library
Graham Marley
C. Marriott
Miss Sarah Medlam
Mr. J.P. Meyer
Richard Miles
Luke Millar
Mr. Ian Miller
Roy Miller
Millers Antiques
Mr. R.M. Milligan
Patrick C. Moore
C. Morley
Mr. John G. Morris

Messrs. Ralph & Bruce Moss
Mr. Frederick Mulherron
Mrs. Ursula Muncaster
Dr. Tessa Murdoch
D. Murphy, Esq.
Mrs. C.C. Murray-Philipson

National Art Library, Victoria & Albert
  Museum
National Museums & Galleries on
  Merseyside
National Museum of Wales
The Nelson-Atkins Museum of Art,
  Kansas City
New Abbey Antiques
Mr. John Newman
J. Michael Nolte
The Duke of Norfolk, K.G.,
  G.C.V.O., C.B., C.B.E., M.C.
Michael Norman Antiques
Paul Northwood

Mr. Howard David Oldroyd
Mrs. P. Onions (West Dean College)
Mr. C.E. Osborne
Mrs. Pamela Osborne
Mr. C.S. Overton

Florian Papp, Inc.
Mr. B.F.J. Pardoe
Michael Pashby
Tim Payne, B.Sc., A.R.I.C.S.
Pelham Galleries
Mr. T.L. Phelps
Phillips of Hitchin (Antiques) Ltd.
Phillips Son & Neale
David Pickup
Mr. Keith Pinn
Colin Piper
Mrs. Sue R. Pittman
Anthony Pratt Fine Arts Ltd.
Sumpter T. Priddy, III, Inc.
Sebastian Pryke, Esq.
Queen Mary & Westfield College Library
Dr. & Mrs. J. Raine
Mr. P.J. Rankin
Mrs. F. Raven
Mr. Piers Raymond
Simon Redburn
Mr. Dick Reid
Miss Rosemary Rendel
Simon Reynolds
S.J. Richmond-Watson, Esq.
William Rieder
Ms. Noël Riley

Mrs. Caroline Rimell
H.A. Roberts
Godfrey Robertson
Mr. Keith Robinson
Treve Rosoman
Mr. W.B. Rouse
Mrs. A. Russett
Jeremy Rye

St. Andrews University Library
Moise Y. Safra
Patrick Sandberg
Dr. Eberhard Sasse
E.A. Saunders, Esq.
Emil Schneeberg
Mr. Kevin Scott
John Seagrim
Mary Shand
Mr. Mark A.C. Shanks
Oliver Shanks, Esq.
Lady Shaw Stewart
Mrs. Sheffield
Anthony Short
Mr. Nicholas Sibley
John Silk
Michael Sim
Mr. M. Simkins
Miss Victoria Slowe
Mr. Adrian M. Smith
Mrs. Barbara M. Smith
W. John Smith, M.A., F.S.A.
Nicholas Somers, Esq., F.S.V.A.
Sotheby's Furniture Department,
New York
Dr. G. Spoto
Mr. Tim Squire-Sanders
Dr. John Stabler
Mrs. Carole Statham-Fletcher
Mrs. Anne Stevens
Mr. Christopher Claxton Stevens
Mr. Colin Stock
Glynn Stockdale
The Hon. Georgina Stonor
T.J. Strevens
Susan Stuart
Mr. R.J. Styles
W. Sutton
Mrs. Margaret Swain, M.B.E.
Miss Marilyn Swain

G.E. Sworder & Sons
Mr. Geoffrey H. Sykes
L.M. Synge, Esq.

H.R. Tempest
M.S. Thomas
Mr. N.W. Thomas
The Rev. Henry Thorold, F.S.A.
James Todd
Treen Antiques
Trist & McBain (Edinburgh)
Mr. J.C.B. Turner
M. Turpin
Dr. Thomas Tuohy

Anthony Verschoyle
Museum of Applied Arts Library, Vienna

Mrs. F.M. Waddington
Dr. Peter Wakely
Jorge Portuondo Wakonigg
John Walker
Patrick Walker, O.B.E.
J.B. Walsby
Graham Watson
Dr. J. Philip L. Welch
Welsh Folk Museum, St. Fagans
John A. Werwaiss
H. Whitbread
Elizabeth White
Christopher Wilk
Mr. J. Anthony Williams
Martin Williams
Robert Williams
Richard Wills, Esq.
Roger D. Wilson
Wilsons Antiques
Printed Book & Periodical Collection,
Winterthur Library
Michael Wisehall, Esq.
Mr. T. Wonnacott
Jeremy R. Wood
Miss Lucy Wood
Thomas Woodcock, Esq.
Mr. Shaun A. Woodward
M.C.A. Wyvill, Esq.

John Young & Son (Antiques)

INTRODUCTION

Gillows of Lancaster and London were one of the great cabinet-making firms of the late eighteenth and nineteenth centuries. If this statement appears partisan to some readers, I can only say that my forthcoming monograph on *Gillow Furniture* will thoroughly document the assessment, and observe meanwhile that even the Lancaster branch counted no fewer than nine dukes on its books in the early nineteenth century. Why, then, is their name not better known? For Gillow is no longer a household word as are Chippendale, Sheraton, and Hepplewhite. There are three obvious reasons why this is so. First, Gillows never published a book of furniture designs to which their name would have been attached. Second, their name has been associated with 'Waring &'. Towards the end of the nineteenth century Gillows' remarkable expansion was faltering in unfavourable economic conditions, and their amalgamation with the Liverpool firm of Waring in 1897[1] diverted them from the admirable standard of furniture-making and interior decoration which they had maintained previously, even after the withdrawal of the Gillow family from the business between 1813 and 1820[2]. Waring & Gillow were nevertheless of international importance as interior designers and decorators (notably of hotels, theatres, private houses, luxury liners and yachts) during the Edwardian years and even later. The company was dissolved in 1938[3] but its name was unfortunately perpetuated in a chain of 'Waring & Gillow' shops, sporting a bogus claim to have been established in 1695 and displaying bastard forms of reproduction furniture, which occupied prominent sites in many a town and city until recently. Dealers in fine English furniture were faced with a dilemma: what to do about the GILLOWS.LANCASTER mark, once so proudly impressed on much of that branch's output[4]. Gillows was redolent of 'Waring &'; and Lancaster — a provincial place, somewhere 'up North'. The solution for some, at least, was to excise the mark[5] and, having discreetly filled in the gap, to market the piece as 'Sheraton', 'Hepplewhite', or even 'Adam'. At the present time there is no telling how many items have been thus doctored, but it seems likely that the practice was sufficiently widespread to distort our assessment of Gillows.

The third reason for Gillows' relative obscurity in this century is that so much furniture supplied by the firm has been sold away from its original location. This can be said of much other furniture, of course, but it is especially so in the case of this firm on two accounts. In addition to the general dispersals of country house contents, many of the houses furnished by Gillows in North Wales, Cheshire, and above all in Lancashire have been the victims of creeping industrialization and other disasters which caused owners to sell and move. The second point is even more important, for it applies to all parts of the country. Much Gillow furniture was small in scale, elegant in line, and fine in quality of timber and workmanship: it was therefore always in demand, even in the last century. However, it was sold not as Gillow but as Sheraton or Hepplewhite.

Gillows' contemporaries, however, viewed the firm very favourably indeed.

Auctioneers habitually garnished their descriptions of lots as 'by that excellent maker Mr. Gillow', and this was as true of London firms as it was of local ones in Liverpool[6]. Distinguished clients flocked to Gillows: the firm's involvement in furnishing so many notable houses, especially in the early nineteenth century (Belvoir Castle is the latest to be documented) demonstrates that the observation about their being the most eminent in the capital[7] was not wide of the mark. And yet the question remains: why have Chippendale, Sheraton, and Hepplewhite lent their names to major furniture styles — but not Gillows? The fundamental reason is that Gillows did not see fit to publish a pattern-book. Moreover the Gillow records were seen by very few eyes prior to their acquisition by Westminster City Libraries in December 1966. At that time Gillows' name was, of course, known among leading auctioneers, dealers, scholars and, not least, Lancastrians. Since I began work on the archive much has changed. A flawed article on the famous suite of furniture from Workington Hall has been corrected.[8] The pioneering publication on Gillows' clock-cases has been supplemented by more detailed work linking the firm's sketches to actual pieces.[9] Some of the important furniture at Tatton Park was examined in detail.[10] Detective work, piecing together information from various parts of the Gillow Archive (see below, p. 20–1) enabled a superb set of chairs to be traced to an order from Robert Parker of Halifax in 1790[11], and a pair of fine elliptical commodes (in the Courtauld Institute's Galleries) to Sir Roger Newdigate of Arbury Hall in 1788[12]. Gillows' designs for altars and other religious items supplied to their fellow-Catholics (a group of major importance in the web of patronage that sustained the firm) have recently been described and illustrated[13]. A start has been made on analysing the firm's trade with the West Indies[14] from whence came most of the fine woods for which it was famous.

Gillow furniture can be seen in leading museums — for example in London, Leeds, Adelaide, Melbourne, and Auckland. However, its systematic collection was pioneered by Abbot Hall Art Gallery in Kendal from its foundation in 1962. A Gillow Museum was established in Lancaster in 1976; although handicapped by a late start it has succeeded in acquiring some interesting and important pieces, notably the library table originally made for Denton Hall, Yorkshire, in 1778.

Much, then, has changed in the last twenty-five years and the status of Gillows has risen considerably. Not only do leading auctioneers now highlight Gillow items but also 'in the manner of Gillow' has become commonplace. And yet we have hardly exposed the tip of an enormous iceberg. For the Gillow Archive *is* enormous: the Estimate Sketch Books, from which most of this book is taken, are only a fraction of the whole. Most users of the archive have sampled them, often with lopsided results owing to neglect of other material, notably the Waste Books. For the full story of Gillows' Lancaster branch it is necessary to interweave material from the whole range of the Archive. This, together with such information as can be recovered about the Oxford Street branch from private archives (there being virtually no Gillow Archive for

London), combined with extensive fieldwork to trace and photograph extant furniture, will form a much larger book on *Gillow Furniture* by the present writer which is well advanced on its path to publication. Meanwhile the rich mine of the Estimate Sketch Books has been available only to those who have access to the microfilms. The purpose of this book is to make available the essence of these sketches to a wider readership; a second volume covering the years 1800 to 1840 is planned. The cut-off date 1800 is more than a convenient round figure for it marks the retirement from business of Richard Gillow, the genius of the firm (see below pp. 19–20).

Wider knowledge of these sketches and designs will serve a variety of purposes. They cannot fail to inform and inspire those who are in any way involved with teaching and researching in furniture history, as well as those who buy and sell such furniture. Some readers will recognize items that can be matched with the original client and traced through family ownership. I should be very pleased to hear of such information and add it to my extensive files which combine data from the Gillow records, and from bank and family archives, with information from museums, dealers, and auctioneers. The point cannot be too strongly emphasized that cumulative data create a 'ripple effect' – that is, unsuspected connections can be identified and suspected connections firmly established. Above all these sketches and drawings will place Gillows in a clearer perspective vis-a-vis the well-known eighteenth-century pattern-books. The words of Percy Macquoid to the effect that much of the inlaid and satinwood furniture generally attributed to Hepplewhite, Shearer, and Sheraton might be the work of Gillows[15] were prophetic, for this is evidently so. In addition to the growth in knowledge and the shift in emphasis over the last twenty-five years already mentioned, Sheraton and Hepplewhite in particular have come to be regarded as mere reporters rather than originators of furniture designs[16]. Indeed, Sheraton was recently described as a plagiarising author[17]. It is more than likely that Gillows' London showrooms provided material for him and for Hepplewhite.

The question of originality in furniture design is both difficult and largely unsolvable. Here it is enough to remark that Sheraton's *The Cabinet-Maker and Upholsterer's Drawing-Book* (1793)[18] consists largely of pedantic rules and observations on drawing, both geometrical and perspective; there are 350 pages of this as opposed to 96 (or 156 if the Appendix is included) on furniture. Hepplewhite's *The Cabinet-Maker and Upholsterer's Guide* (1788) does at least consist of plates and text about furniture, but his authorship and standing have been judged and found wanting[19]. After 1793 Sheraton did not practise as a cabinet-maker; Hepplewhite was connected with a modest business in Cripplegate, of which nothing is known and from which no piece of furniture has been traced: if he was indeed a manufacturer, as opposed to a mere retailer, he must have been insignificant. And yet these patternbooks found a public: the *Guide* had a second edition in 1789 and a third in 1794; the *Drawing-Book's* second edition came out in 1794 and its third in 1802. Who wanted them? Clearly, in an increasingly populous and prosperous Britain there was a large and growing number of customers for furniture as well as cabinet-makers to serve them. Gillows in particular rose to the challenge: their 'spectacular success' has been attributed to their massive and unprecedented production[20]. For example, the Lancaster branch made over 1100 chairs in 1792[21]. Publications such as these supplied a pool of ideas into which both clients and cabinet-makers were free to dip. It is significant that one customer who asked Gillows to make an item which he had seen in the *Guide* was told firmly that they did not own a copy[22]. They did subscribe to the first edition of the *Drawing-Book* but not to Sheraton's subsequent books, which is also significant. In any case Gillows had their own internal designs and designers. Although the designers at the London branch remain anonymous they produced a steady stream of drawings for the Lancaster firm; at Lancaster Richard Gillow, William Beckett and Thomas Romney among others were involved in designing. Gillows certainly appear to have borrowed the occasional design from Sheraton – such was the point of subscribing to publications – but it seems likely that Sheraton took more from Gillows than they did from him[23]. Precocious neo-classical features which might once have been called 'Sheraton' can be found in Gillow designs as early as 1767 and 1770[24]. The huge range of Gillows' designs was never published; on the contrary, their confidentiality was jealously guarded. The explanation is that there *was* a Gillow style (see below, pp. 25–30) and the partners wanted to preserve its exclusivity as far as possible. Clients to whom Gillows entrusted designs were routinely exhorted not to allow them to be seen by anyone in the furniture trade. Of course, there were chinks in their armour: with professional plagiarists like Sheraton (by his own admission)[25] and Hepplewhite (by inference) doing the rounds of leading shops in London, memorising salient design features, and returning home to sketch them with an eye to publication, it was impossible to exclude every potential competitor and pirate. After all, Richard Gillow himself had observed a 'horse-shoe' table at another cabinet-maker's when such objects were novel and sketched it for his own ends[26].

The Firm of Gillows

From modest beginnings in provincial Lancaster the Gillow family forged ahead: by the third quarter of the century their London shop and manufactory, established in 1769, was prominent among the capital's cabinet-making firms, and from about the turn of the century its pre-eminence was reflected in the great number of London mansions and country houses which it provided with furniture, upholstery, and maintenance[27].

The firm was founded in Lancaster about 1730[28] by Robert Gillow the elder (1704–1772) who had served his apprenticeship there and taken out his freedom of the borough in the mayoral year 1727–28. At that time Lancaster was emerging from the chrysalis-like state which it had maintained during the seventeenth century. Then a place of only modest and fluctuating prosperity, based on its regional importance and coasting trade, it was now beginning to look westwards across the Atlantic to the Caribbean islands[29]. Jamaica and Barbados in particular offered both a supply of cotton, sugar, rum, and fine timber and a market for finished manufactures from the North and Midlands: these included textiles, clothes, shoes, and furniture. In common with other entrepreneurs of this generation, Robert Gillow was intent on building up capital by living modestly and ploughing back profits into the business. He came of a yeoman family which, although of modest means (latterly, at any rate), was able and proud to trace its ancestry through many generations of devout Catholics both before and after the Reformation. Above all, to judge by its eighteenth-century members, the Gillow family was of high intelligence. These qualities added up to an ideal specification for an ambitious young businessman in the early eighteenth century: he had the incentive to make money in a period of expansion during Walpole's long and stable regime, the drive to make his mark quickly in Lancaster and beyond at a time when the town was beginning to experience exceptional prosperity, and the additional spur of being a member of the Catholic minority. Catholicism meant exclusion from any participation in public life but perfect freedom to engage in business. In the Gillow family's case it also presented them with a ready-made clientele among the Catholic gentry and nobility, not only in the North but throughout England as well as Scotland and Ireland. That is to anticipate, however, for it was in the second generation that the business expanded so dramatically.

Robert Gillow the elder had several sons, of whom two were crucial to the firm's successful growth. Richard (1733–1811), the eldest, was to become the most gifted of all the Gillows. His early years are not well documented but it is certain that he spent some time in Barbados, and very probable that he had some architectural training in London with William Jones[30]. From 1757 he was in partnership with his father (until the latter's retirement in 1769) and, although he was well acquainted with London, he remained at the head of the Lancaster business until his own retirement at the end of the century. His younger brother Robert II (1747–1795) might well have continued as he began, that is by reinforcing the Lancaster management, but Providence determined otherwise. The Gillows had contemplated a direct link with the capital, which dominated the furniture trade, for some time but it was in 1769 that a London branch was opened with Thomas Gillow (a cousin) and William Taylor (who had trained as a cabinet-maker in Lancaster) as partners. Although there were sound reasons, including the fear of bankruptcy, for keeping the Lancaster and London businesses technically separate, in practice they operated closely in many respects. In particular, Lancaster was well placed to exploit its ample supplies of timber and relatively low wages to build up a profitable 'export' trade to London by sea and also by land. The death of William Taylor in 1775 meant that Thomas Gillow needed another partner and it fell to Robert to move to London. Thomas Gillow then died in 1779, leaving Robert as the mainstay until Richard's three sons were old enough to become partners[31]. Since the surviving records are (with one exception, an upholstery jobbing-book[32]) those of the Lancaster branch, little is known about the London end. Occasional references to furniture made in Lancaster for Robert's clients (for instance Lady Clifford of Chudleigh and Lord Arundell of Wardour, both prominent Catholics) provide clues that can only be followed up in the archives of the families in question. When such links have been traced significant information has emerged. It is clear that from the beginning Gillows in London were patronized by leading members of the gentry and aristocracy and that the firm ranked high among metropolitan cabinet-makers. Two obvious factors help account for its success: Richard Gillow devoted a good deal of time to supervising its management in the vital early stages, and he left no stone unturned to direct potential customers, especially influential ones, toward the new enterprise; and Robert was a great friend of the architect Samuel Wyatt, an alliance that brought numerous important commissions for furnishing country houses[33] and at the same time raised Gillows' standards of design to an entirely new and superior level. The earliest example of this collaboration known to me is their work at Heaton House (now Hall) in the 1770s, where the Lancaster branch provided the dining-room chairs and their London colleagues made the splendid saloon chairs. The latter were not the only Gillow chairs which have been attributed to the Linnells. However, the ethos and economics of furniture design were changing. The magnificent carved and gilded pieces (pier-glasses and tables, for instance) of the Chippendale period, were beginning to seem costly, outmoded, and ponderous. Wyatt-Gillow furniture was more modern in the sense of being fine but not wildly luxurious. It is increasingly clear that in furniture, as in architecture, the influence of the Wyatts (both James and Samuel, but especially Samuel) was of the greatest importance during the late eighteenth century. At the risk of over-simplifying, I would say that their great rival Robert Adam designed furniture which tended to be encrusted with ornament and gilding to the detriment of its line[34]. To the Wyatts, famous for the sober restraint and even austerity of their interiors, I attribute the severe geometrical line and form, using the minimum of ornament, gilding, and inlay and maximising the beauty of fine woods, that is unquestionably the hallmark of the best Gillow furniture of the last quarter of the eighteenth century, and which is clearly seen in many of the designs reproduced in this book.

The Gillow Designs

The most obvious feature of the Gillow designs is the wide variation in finish (or lack of it) that prevails among the thousands of sketches and drawings. The reason is that these designs were not worked up for publication but, on the contrary, were either part of the firm's private business records or intended for their customers' *confidential* perusal. It is important for the reader to understand something of the scope of the Gillow Archive (now at the City of Westminster Archives Centre, 10 St. Ann's Street, London SW1P 2XR). This has been called incomparable[35] and rightly so, since nothing like it survives as documentation for the history of English furniture before 1824, when the Holland Archive —

which contains no drawings[36] − begins, and it is virtually certain that nothing like it will surface in future. The Gillow Archive comprises 197 volumes for the period from 1731 to 1932; of these, 80 are before 1830 including letter-books, ledgers, waste-books (records of daily transactions)[37], and estimate sketch books. The estimate sketch books begin in 1784 and continue until 1899; they contain some 20,000 items[38]. This selection has been made from volumes covering the years 1784 to 1800[39], augmented by some earlier sketches[40], by a price agreement which contains designs for chairs not otherwise represented[41], and by a few of the finished designs that were meant for the eyes of prospective customers[42]. The draughtsmanship varies greatly, even among the finished drawings. The representation of figures, both animal and human, is frankly poor (e.g. Figs. 205, 214). However, most of the drawings are of an acceptable standard, and some are better than that, such as the girandoles in Figs. 203, 210, 218, and 221.

Unlike the finished drawings, the Estimate Sketch Books were intended purely for the firm's internal purposes, which were twofold. In the first place they functioned as their collective memory for a variety of needs: for example, a customer might wish to re-order an item, either bought by himself or seen at a friend's house, which had been supplied some years previously; in such cases the firm would need not only to pinpoint the appearance of the piece but also to adjust its costing to take account of fluctuations in the price of materials − usually, but not always, upwards. The other component in pricing was, of course, labour and this invariably went up − not annually but from time to time when the men wrested an increase from their employers. It is surely not mere coincidence that the main series of estimate sketch books begins in 1784, a time when a major re-negotiation of wages was in progress[43]. In consequence the employers kept a detailed record of wage costs which forms part of the estimate in most cases: indeed, the annotations often encroach on the sketch to the detriment of its visual appeal. In any case the visual quality varies. Sometimes we have a minute thumbnail sketch which is, nevertheless, of interest because of its early date or because it represents an important clue towards tracking down actual Gillow furniture. This is particularly applicable in the early period up to 1770 or so, when a mere squiggle does duty for a rococo fielded panel or elaborate cresting (see below, pp. 25−26). During the period from 1770 to 1800 − the era of Gillows' classic furniture − the sketches tend to be more ambitious but stronger on outline then detail. However, a minority are carefully detailed and shaded in wash, an offshoot perhaps of the grey or colour-wash drawings prepared for customers. The volume of prices for workmanship stands apart: it was obviously not for the eyes of customers but, on the other hand, the numbered chair designs are evidently related to corresponding ones that *were* sent out by post or messenger. Some of these are executed in a style reminiscent of contemporary silhouettes.

The importance of these sketches is, therefore, threefold. (1) They are a factual record of furniture produced by Gillows, usually with valuable information about the cost of materials, workmanship, the craftsman or men responsible, and the client for whom the piece was made; sometimes there is also an order number after that system was introduced in 1785. (2) Since they relate to actual furniture, any item is theoretically traceable: a good example is the commode (Fig. 121) which was made for Sir Roger Newdigate and is now in the Courtauld Institute's Galleries. In practice, of course, it is not so easy: although a vast amount of the furniture survives, much has been bequeathed or sold by the original families. On the other hand, a good deal still remains with some families' descendants and such success as I have had in tracing examples will appear in my forthcoming book on *Gillow Furniture*. Others will no doubt pursue the trail: the index of personal names in Part Two of this book is the starting-point. (3) The sketches and drawings were unpublished and confidential: in the case of finished designs sent out to clients the recipient was almost always enjoined to take care that the drawings were not shown to others and especially not to rival cabinet-makers. They were, in effect, trade secrets and the implication is clear enough: these were individual designs, of which Gillows were both proud and jealous. Consequently they have an importance quite different from the published designs of Chippendale, Hepplewhite, Sheraton, and others which were a lake in which anyone might fish. Chippendale is the most significant comparison for he was both head of a cabinet-making firm and author of the *Gentleman and Cabinet-Maker's Director*. Much ink has been wasted on attempts to link extant furniture that corresponds with his designs to his firm, but in vain, for once published, the designs were anyone's. Gillows, on the other hand, chose to keep their designs to themselves and it does follow that furniture closely matching these is most probably theirs. A degree of caution is in order since it was impossible to prevent a visitor to the showroom from sketching an item when he returned home and commissioning a cheaper version elsewhere or, if he were a cabinet-maker, from executing it himself. It may be doubted whether this happened in practice, at least to any significant degree. In any case the assessment of Gillow furniture depends not only on style but also on the quality of wood and workmanship: when all three are satisfactorily present the judgment is usually not in doubt. The other important ingredient is family provenance. My own assessment of Gillow furniture is founded on pieces which are documented in the Estimate Sketch Books and/or the Waste Books: once an unshakeable base has been established, it becomes realistic to extend the inquiry to partially documented items, e.g. where a proven family connection with Gillows exists but there is no surviving documentation for the piece in question. The Gillow records demonstrate how certain families, and not only Catholic ones, remained loyal to the firm over many years, in some cases for three generations. An excellent example is the Catholic Tempest family of Broughton Hall near Skipton, which first patronised Gillows in 1763 and was still buying in the 1840s. Broughton Hall's collection of Gillow furniture has long been recognized as outstanding and although the house is not open to the public on a regular basis it can be studied in published works[44]. The Egertons of Tatton Park near Knutsford likewise patronised Gillows from 1780 at least until the

1830s. They were not Catholics but they do represent another major strand in the Gillow story in that they employed a succession of Wyatts as architects[45]. Tatton Park is a National Trust property and open to the public; it ranks as one of the best collections of Gillow furniture still in the house for which it was designed. Some of its furniture, mainly bedroom pieces, has been published in detail[46], but there is a great deal more in the house, which is particularly rich in early nineteenth-century items.

The Social Dimension

The Estimate Sketch Books illuminate several aspects of Georgian social life, sometimes in unexpected ways. Gillows' Catholic loyalties brought them numerous commissions for altars, altarpieces, tabernacles, and crucifixes as well as a font and a pulpit[47]. Their business was founded, in addition to cabinet-making, on building and joinery, which is indicated in such articles as doors, pillars, pilasters, portals, quoins, scrolls for window architraves, and — the never-fail moneyspinner — coffins[48]. Industry is represented by a loom for weaving hair cloth. The running of a household demanded airing, clothes, and linen horses as well as napkin presses; also bone tubs, boot and shoe horses, foot brushes, green warmers, hasters[49] (for keeping meat hot), flowerstands, kitchen stands and chairs[50], mangles[51], meat safes, and toasting forks. Medicine chests were a sure indication of the current trend towards self-doctoring[52]. Powdering-closets remind us that both sexes powdered their hair liberally. For pets there were bird and squirrel cages, and a stool for a dog. For pastimes and exercise we find bow and arrow cases and gun cases; backgammon boxes and tables as well as the obvious card tables; billiard and troumadam tables, chamber horses, a camera obscura; paint boxes, drawing boxes, desks and stands. 'Lucets', unknown to the *Oxford English Dictionary*, appear to have been frames for some kind of feminine handwork.

One of the most interesting aspects of Gillows' business is the wide spectrum of their clientele. In addition to the gentry and aristocracy (see below, pp. 24–5) the Estimate Sketch Books record sales to tradesmen including bellman, book-seller, cabinet-maker, chandler, cooper, druggist, farrier, grocer, ironmonger, limner, mason, printer, tailor, tinman, tobacconist, and writing-master. Their customers numbered many merchants, some of whom were exporting furniture made by Gillows, for example Calvert, Harrison & Chippindale and Carter, Workswick, Gillow & Co. Industrialists included Robert Peel of Bury, Lancs. and Drayton Manor, Staffs., Henry Sudell of Woodfold Park, Blackburn, and presumably Cromptons, Kays, and Shuttleworths. Among West Indies clients were the Hon. William Payne Georges, Chief Justice of St. Kitts and, retired to England, Moses Benson who bought superb furniture. Many, perhaps most, of those styled 'Captain' were mariners who sailed the ships in which Gillows' furniture and other goods were exported, but at least one was an officer of the 20th Regiment and another named Napier and styled 'the Hon.' must have been outside this group. A good number of majors, colonels, and a general filled the military complement. Among other professions, which included a couple of bankers of whom Hugh Hoare was one, the law, medicine, and the church were well represented. Among the lawyers we may note a good sprinkling of attorneys with some more prominent individuals such as Charles Gibson, Deputy Protonotary, of Myerscough House and Quernmore Park; Henry Tomkinson of Dorfold Hall; and a judge, Alan Chambre (later knighted), of Abbot Hall. There were rather more doctors, and many clergymen. A few of the clergy were Catholics — the Rev. Joseph Laurence Hadley was a prominent Benedictine and the Rev. Dr. John Rigby was the parish priest in Lancaster — but the majority were Anglican. It is beyond the scope of this essay to determine their status within the Established Church, but some were clearly 'gentry', such as the Rev. Fergus Graham of Arthuret, Longtown and the Rev. Sir William Clarke, Bt., Fellow of All Souls College, Oxford and Rector of Bury, Lancs. A brace of deans (Carlisle and St. Asaph) were capped by four bishops (Carlisle, Durham, Gloucester, Llandaff) and the Archbishop of York.

The spectrum becomes more interesting as the subjects rise in the social hierarchy — not for snobbish reasons but because the gentry and aristocracy inevitably spent more than tradesmen and the minor professional men, their families (if not always their houses) usually survive, and often their descendants still own some of the furniture commissioned by their forbears. Among many gentry families the following were notable as Catholics: the Cliffords of Tixall, the Cliftons of Lytham Hall, the Constables of Terregles House, the Fitzherbert-Brockholeses of Claughton Hall, the Fitzherberts of Swynnerton Park, the Giffards of Chillington Hall, the Heneages of Hainton Hall, the Howards of Corby Castle, the Stonors of Stonor Park, the Stricklands of Sizergh Hall (now Castle), the Tempests of Broughton Hall, the Traffords of Trafford Park, and the Welds of Britwell. Two other notable recusant families appear not in the Estimate Sketch Books but in the Waste Books: the Blundells of Ince and the Welds of Stonyhurst and Lulworth. The Ansons of Shugborough Manor, the Bankeses of Winstanley Hall, the Biglands of Bigland Hall, the Christians (later Christian-Curwens) of Workington Hall and Belle Isle, and the Egertons of Tatton Park all belonged to the Established Church. The baronets were Sir Walter Blount of Mawley Hall, Salop, Sir John Brisco of Crofton Place, Cumberland, Sir Richard Brooke of Norton Priory, Cheshire, Sir John Chetwode of Brand Hall, Staffs. (now Salop), the Rev. Sir William Clarke 'near Bury', Lancs., Sir Thomas Egerton of Heaton House near Manchester (later Baron Grey de Wilton), Sir Thomas Frankland of Thirkleby Park, Yorks., Sir Thomas Gage of Hengrave Hall, Suffolk, Sir James Gardiner of Clerk Hill, Lancs., Sir William Gerard of Garswood Hall, Lancs., Sir James Graham of Netherby Hall, Cumberland, Sir Thomas Hesketh of Rufford New Hall, Lancs., Sir Henry Hoghton of Walton Hall, Lancs., Sir James Ibbetson of Denton Hall, Yorks., Sir John Lawson of Brough Hall, Yorks., Sir Wilfred Lawson of Brayton Hall, Cumberland, Sir Michael Le Fleming of Rydal Hall, Westmorland, Sir John Leicester of Tabley Hall, Cheshire, Sir William Milner of Nun Appleton Hall, Yorks., Sir Roger

Newdigate of Arbury Hall, Warwickshire, Sir John Ramsden of Byram Hall, Yorks., Sir John Stanley of Hoylake, Cheshire, Sir William Stanley of Hooton Hall, Cheshire, Sir John Shaw Stewart of Ardgowan, Renfrewshire, and Sir John Borlase Warren of Stapleford Hall, Leicestershire.

Next on the social ladder came a group of sons of the nobility bearing the courtesy title 'Lord': Frederick and George Cavendish of Holker Hall, Lord Garlies of Galloway House, heir to the Earl of Galloway, Archibald Hamilton of Ashton Hall, Lancaster, also Suffolk and London, later ninth Duke of Hamilton, and Archibald Montgomerie of Coilsfield, Ayrshire, heir to the Earldom of Eglinton. Then the barons: Lords Grenville, Grey de Wilton, Harrowby, Milford, Muncaster, and Stourton. Viscount Montagu was the sole representative of that rank, but he was followed by a covey of earls: the twelfth Earl of Derby, the fourth Earl of Effingham, the twelfth Earl of Eglinton, the seventh Earl Ferrers, the seventh Earl of Galloway, the second Earl of Ilchester, the eighth Earl of Lauderdale, the fifth Earl of Rochford, the fifteenth Earl of Shrewsbury, the fifth Earl of Shaftesbury, and the fifth Earl of Strafford. Finally there was a brace of dukes: the fourth Duke of Atholl and the ninth of Hamilton. Among these grandees the Scottish connection which was so important in Gillows' business was represented by Atholl, Eglinton, Galloway, Hamilton, and Lauderdale. Derby was, of course, a leading figure in the North-West of England and as such he represented the patronage of that region which was, like that of the Catholics (here personified in Shrewsbury), fundamental to the firm's rise to greatness.

The Gillow Style

Although the main series of Estimate Sketch Books begins only in 1784 there are a few sketches which enable us to glimpse something of the Gillow style in the 1760s and even earlier. Cabriole legs of an early Georgian type survive in a universal table of 1769 (Fig. 3) and a settee of about 1761 (Fig. 243). Rococo motifs were employed during the 1760s to the extent of scrolled toes, carved claws, and fretted galleries on tea tables (Figs. 70–73) and scrolled toes (or perhaps pad feet) can be seen on a corner table (Fig. 52). The last of the group of tea-tables, entirely a-typical for its date (1786), was probably the taste of the Hamburg client who ordered it but it gives an excellent idea of the firm's earlier style. The pier-glass in Fig. 197 also harks back to the '50s or even '40s: again, its late appearance in 1771 was probably a whim of the Antigua resident for whom it was made. Serpentine-framed panels on the 'large Piece of Furniture' dated 1766 (Fig. 133) could be ascribed to Gillows' conservative instincts but again it is possible that it was a special order, particularly in view of the ambiguity of its description. However, a serpentine commode chest of drawers of 1789 (Fig. 117) was destined for the London shop and at that date it can only mean that enough conservative customers in the capital liked the design: it is a caution against supposing that everyone followed the latest trend.

The Gillow style of the 1760s can be visualised from a dozen or so sketches.

At floor level the swelled ogee foot long remained a Gillow feature (Figs. 25, 133, 193, 294–6). At the top, carcase furniture was often crowned with a pediment, either open or scrolled, frequently with a carved 'shield' or cartouche or a bust in the centre (e.g. Figs. 110, 124–5, 134, 139, 142, 165, 172–3). As late as 1797 a library bookcase bore closed pediments that were quite typical and which presumably exemplify Richard Gillow's architectural knowledge acquired during the years when Palladianism ruled supreme (Fig. 168). So, too, do the Vitruvian scrolls that appear on a table-frame (not illustrated[53]) and, less conventionally, in the border of a bureau-bookcase (Fig. 140). Between top and bottom of a piece there might be carved friezes (e.g. Fig. 133) and frets (e.g. Fig. 137), carved spandrels (Fig. 172), carved brackets in the angles where the legs joined the carcase (Figs. 124–5, 180) or supporting a bookshelf (Figs. 160–1), and carved splats on chairs and settees (Figs. 243, 249). Both the smoking chair (Fig. 244) and the reading-chair (Fig. 246) were late examples of types that go back to the 1740s in the Gillow records. A pier-glass design of that period was resurrected in 1790 (Fig. 198) and the familiar carved frets of the mid-century pier-glass (often enriched with gilt birds &c) likewise experienced a second coming (Fig. 199). Both were destined for export to the West Indies, and both were exceptional for their date.

A distinctively English contribution to eighteenth-century furniture was the Gothick style, and Gillows adopted it in their habitually restrained manner. The cluster-column legs of card and universal tables (Figs. 1–2); bed-pillars with quatrefoils (Fig. 103); and the spires and pinnacles roughly indicated in the cresting of the 'large Piece' already mentioned (Fig. 133) all speak of modified Strawberry Hill, as does (despite its 1795 date) the battlemented and pinnacled library bookcase (Fig. 170). Later manifestations such as a dressing-glass (Fig. 196), a window cornice with cusps and quatrefoils (Fig. 228), a church screen with 'rose window' and bar tracery (Fig. 171), glazing-bars in bookcases (Figs. 139–40, 156, 158, 166), albeit juxtaposed with classical pediments (e.g. Fig. 166), proclaim rather the world of Northanger Abbey.

When writing about the furniture of the 1760s the term 'transitional' creeps in sooner or later and in the case of Gillows it seems appropriate to apply it to the pedestal carved with four festoons, apparently of flowers and/or foliage, dated 1767 (Fig. 176); to the slender cabinets on tapering legs, dated 1768 and 1770 (Figs. 124–5) which foretell the light and elegant style prevalent from the 1770s to the 1790s; and to the 'hollow corners' (in which carved roses were applied) in the astragal mouldings that defined panels (e.g. Figs. 82, 98, 137, 164, 176, 179, 181, 190) which were a standard motif on transitional and neo-classical furniture.

Neo-classicism dominated Gillow furniture during the 1770s, 1780s, and 1790s. It took more than one form. In the first place the firm employed the whole gamut of motifs that stocked the common pool from which all designers selected. Nowhere is this seen more clearly than in the range of elegant girandoles and pier-glasses (especially Figs. 202–3, 212, 215, 218). These drew on arabesques (Figs. 200, 202, 218, 227), drapery (e.g. Figs. 208, 220) festoons (e.g. Fig. 202), flowers and foliage (Figs. 203–4, 208, 210, 212, 215, 220–1), palmette and anthemion (e.g. Figs. 200, 213), cornucopias (e.g. Fig. 208), rams' heads (e.g. Fig. 217), paterae (e.g. Fig. 63 and *passim*), plumes of feathers (e.g. Figs. 104, 108), tripods (e.g. Figs. 210–212 and cf. 217), vases (e.g. Figs. 79, 85, 109, 210–12, 215, 218, 220–1), and waterleaves which are sometimes indistinguishable from feathers in the sketches (e.g. Figs. 26, 63, 87, 89–91, 178, 190, 217, 227). A trophy of musical instruments japanned on the cupboard of a dressing-table was presumably for a music-loving client; for the classically-minded (or, more probably, simply as a conventional allusion) chaste Diana gazed at her stags on window-cornices (Figs. 36, 227, 231). A wardrobe of good standard design with oval panels was lifted into a higher class by the addition of a fluted gallery with vase or tablet (e.g. Fig. 135). Carving, and inlay – often assisted by engraving (e.g. Fig. 189) – enriched vases (e.g. Figs. 189–90), commodes (e.g. Figs. 119–121 and Colour Plate 12), pier tables (e.g. Fig. 60), and card tables, although the design of Fig. 9 was more elaborate than was usual at the Lancaster manufactory, as was the degree of coloured inlay in Fig. 61. The finer inlaid details are sometimes not shown or not visible in the sketches, for example the paterae in the frieze of Lady Clifford's secretaire-bookcase (Fig. 144). However, there were two sorts of inlaid motif which were constantly used and highly visible. Fans were inlaid, on commodes for instance (Fig. 121 and Colour Plate 12), in the spandrels of sideboards (e.g. Figs. 88, 94), and in segmental or elliptical pediments (e.g. Figs. 145, 161, 166). Flutes were sometimes carved but more often inlaid, as on the base of a cistern (Fig. 178), on the frieze of a pedestal (Fig. 83), on the pillars of a chest of drawers (Fig. 115: 9 per pillar, in black), in the legs of a sideboard (52 of them, Fig. 94 and cf. 93), and in the legs of a breakfast table (Fig. 53). They are too common to note on the legs of seat furniture.

The second form that neo-classicism took with Gillows was closely allied to contemporary developments in architecture: canted bays had their counterparts in hexagonal (e.g. Fig. 128) and octagonal (e.g. Figs. 43, 69, 72, 74, 180) furniture; the bowed and elliptical forms of rooms and windows were fundamental to the architecture of Samuel Wyatt, with whom Gillows had a close connection, and these shapes were no less basic in their furniture. The bow form could disguise a night table (Fig. 102) as well as impart elegance to a commode chest of drawers (Fig. 118) or even a washstand (Fig. 113). The ellipse was used to define bed cornices (Fig. 105) or an ornamental commode (Fig. 120). The bow or ellipse in reverse produced a concave plan. The oval contributed a major shape to chairbacks (e.g. Figs. 253, 255, 268, 270–1). Inlaid oval and circular panels of fine veneer were the principal geometrical form on, for example, bedsteps (Fig. 101), commodes (Fig. 123), wardrobes and low wardrobes (Figs. 130, 135), gardevines (Fig. 182), pedestals (Fig. 192), secretaire-bookcases (Fig. 155), and a library bookcase (Fig. 167). One such design for a pedestal was annotated to the effect that it should have had square, not oval, panels (Fig. 190) an indication of incipient severity. The other geometrical plans that Gillows used extensively and effectively were variations on the convex and concave forms, sometimes juxtaposed against straight lines. Sideboards, for instance, could be concave (Fig. 87), concave and straight (Fig. 86), or concave and convex. The convex-concave-convex shape of a sideboard (Fig. 91) or a dressing-table (Fig. 38) had its own name in Gillows' terminology: 'hollow front & circular ends'.

The severity of some Gillow designs in the late 1780s and 1790s has its counterpart in the architecture of the period, notably that of Henry Holland and Sir John Soane, which profoundly influenced furniture: it is no accident that square-back chairs with straight legs appeared at this time (e.g. Figs. 284−5), or that a bureau-bookcase had astylar pilasters (Fig. 140). However, there was another factor which at first inclined and then impelled cabinet-makers to adopt less extravagant designs: in the last quarter of the century fine timber was, for a variety of reasons, often scarce and therefore costly. The incentive was there to economise. Hence the vogue for painted and japanned furniture constructed of cheap timber, especially beech (e.g. Figs. 10, 17, 128, 170). Hence, too, slender lines and lightness of construction (e.g. Figs. 30, 42−3), even in details such as French and toupie feet e.g. Figs. 102, 113, 117−8, 145−6 (French) and 115, 155, 163 (toupie). However Gillows, ever conscious of practical considerations, refused to go to extremes that equated with flimsiness. In this connection their frequent use of cross-rails or stretchers should be noted (e.g. Figs. 29, 55, 58, 62).

Gillows developed one style, among others, that was quite remarkably 'modern' in its austerity and, I believe, particularly their own. They had already toned down what they evidently regarded as the excessive application of inlaid motifs, which some makers slapped on to such an extent that the lines of the piece were impaired. Gillows, on the contrary, emphasized these lines by a judicious use of contrasting woods in crossbanding, longbanding, 'angles' (edges), and strings both single and double (see notes to figures, *passim*). The shift towards plainness can be seen in the two buffets (Figs. 172, 174) where, among other changes, that dated 1798 had no pediment. The Eglinton bed (Fig. 107) with its footboard was so plain as to foreshadow one aspect of nineteenth-century taste. Some, perhaps many, sideboards were no longer enriched with carved tablets &c. (Figs. 98−9). Some, perhaps many, pier-glasses were now mere rectangles with minimal borders (Fig. 216). The Carus dressing-table had *very* square outlines (Fig. 33). Astragals (glazing-bars) in bookcase doors were often mere intersecting straight lines of the 'lozenge' or diamond type (e.g. Figs. 147, 167). Cornices, which formerly followed closely the cymas, ovolos, and cavettos of the Ionic and Corinthian Orders, now renounced these in favour of the ultra-plain Tuscan or 'new cove' cornice (e.g. Figs. 148, 159, 168). Nor was austerity confined to the reduction or excision of ornament. Economy of line was sometimes matched by economy of function: that is, a given piece could serve as well for one as for another purpose. For example, the Rev. Mr. Hudson's sideboard of 1787 could have been found elsewhere as a dressing-table (Fig. 99). A writing-table was also called a library table by the firm's clerk, who might as well have written dressing table, since it combined the same basic geometrical forms: a concave top on a rectangular base (Figs. 21, 34). A pier table was also called a commode (Fig. 18), a commode was also called a cupboard (Fig. 119) and a sheveret (Figs. 122), and a cupboard was called a commode (Fig. 120).

Finally: how distinctive was Gillows' style? There is no doubt that there was such a style, but care is needed: one can point to features which were used over and over again by Gillows but which were also in general use. Apparently typical pieces of Gillows furniture, such as the buffet, were made throughout the North of England and Scotland. That said, the combination of pediment and shield, swelled ogee (or bracket) feet, and the let-down shelf does add up to a Gillow look. Quintessential Gillow design appears in many types of furniture: card tables (Figs. 5–9), pier tables (Figs. 10–18), pembroke tables (Figs. 60–4), dressing-tables (Figs. 30–4), sideboards (Figs. 83–99), pedestals and vases (Figs. 187–192), gardevines (Figs. 182–3), writing-tables, especially the bureau writing-table (Figs. 24, 27, 39–48), library tables (Figs. 21, 23, 25–7), library bookcases Figs. 166–8 especially), secretaire-bookcases (Figs. 144–8), secretaires and little bookcases (e.g. Fig. 154), secretaires and bookshelves (e.g. Fig. 155), and sheverets (e.g. Fig. 150). Among scores of chair designs these were especially characteristic: drapery and feather (Fig. 273); interlaced hoops carved with wheatears (Fig. 272); the three-upright baluster (Fig. 248); a similar back intended for a dining-chair (Fig. 278); the tablet top-rail (Fig. 286); and the lozenge-back (Fig. 280). These comments are made on the strength of my detailed study of the Waste Books which list almost all Lancaster transactions from 1771 to 1797.

One important Gillow line that cannot be adequately studied from the Estimate Sketch Books is their dining-tables, because the great majority of sketches are mere plans showing the fixed bed and moveable leaves; even elevations usually show little that is distinctive. It should be noted, however, that the oval type (Fig. 51) was also found as a breakfast-table.

Some features that were much used by Gillows were too common to be distinctive in themselves but nevertheless were given a characteristic Gillow look. Such were termed legs (Figs. 93, 96, 125, 149, 179); tablets, on sideboards (Figs. 85, 90–1, 95–7), on window-cornices (Fig. 231), and on card tables (Figs. 6, 9). Such, too, were the shelves beneath items like pier-tables (Figs. 14–5, 17), and the sunk panels in the legs of gardevines (Fig. 182), cisterns (Fig. 179) and sideboards (Figs. 89–90, 95–6). 'Tower corners' (or 'pillars') – the slim, cylindrical members (often fluted) which appeared to support, for instance, a chest of drawers (Fig. 115), a rectangular commode (Fig. 123), or a secretaire-bookcase (Fig. 147) – were yet another form that was widespread in some shape or other but which was certainly characteristic in the way Gillows employed it. As for writing-drawers, as found both in secretaires &c. and in non-writing furniture such as wardrobes (Fig. 132, 135) and library bookcases with wardrobes (Fig. 165), the basic arrangement of pigeon-holes, secret compartments &c. was common enough, but Gillows added variety and interest by their frequent use of pilasters to flank the central arch or door and by the fans which they inlaid on such doors. Within the desk or drawer the 'sliding prospect'[54] or pull-out box was certainly a Gillow speciality (e.g. Figs. 130, 141). The sham-drawer effect, by which a desk or writing-drawer was made to look like two drawers when it was in fact one of double height with a front that let down, was also used generally but Gillows adopted it with such enthusiasm as to have made it their own (e.g. Fig. 144). It may, of course, have been literally their own. A very characteristic Gillow feature was the lettering of compartments within the writing-drawer (not seen in these sketches), or on the outside of drawers in large writing-tables (e.g. Fig. 27). Last but not least Gillows were famous for the quality of the timbers they used. This is the most difficult feature to illustrate from these sketches, of course, and a few squiggles from the pen do duty for the finest veined or flared figures of mahogany or satinwood, such as the 'fine birchings' which gave distinction to an otherwise plain sideboard of 1771 (Fig. 80). Here it is appropriate to emphasise that the term 'birching' or 'birchings' as used by Gillows had nothing to do with birch veneer (never used by them in the eighteenth century): the term invariably referred to the finest figures of mahogany or satinwood.

Such, then, are the principal points of interest in the Gillow Estimate Sketch Books as it appears to me after a lengthy period of studying them. In making this selection I am conscious that many other interesting sketches could have been included if space were not a consideration. However, I believe that the essential features of the Gillow style as practised at Lancaster during the period from 1760 to 1800 are represented here. Those who wish to pursue matters further are referred to the Indexes of Persons, Workmen, and Furniture in Part Two. Finally it remains only to say that I hope that those who read and use this book will share the enjoyment which these sketches and drawings have given me.

Lindsay Boynton
1994

NOTES TO INTRODUCTION

1 The date of the merger is often incorrectly given. To name but a few examples (a) an article in the *Lancaster Guardian* of 9 July, 1993 states 1900 (b) an inquiry at Companies House produced the impossibly late date 1912, with a note that earlier records had been destroyed (c) *A History of Gillow of Lancaster*, by Mary E. Burkett, Edith Tyson, and Davidson How, revised by Rachel Hasted (Lancashire County Museum Service, 1984), p. 22 gives May 1903 without reference. The exact date can be put between 24 June and 16 October 1897: Gillow & Co.'s fire insurance policy with the Scottish Union taken out on the former date was transferred on the latter to Waring & Gillow (information kindly given by Mr. Simon Nuttall in whose possession the policy now is).

2 Following Richard Gillow's death in 1811 a series of changes in the partnership took place which are too complicated to give in full here. Richard Gillow the younger referred on 6 May 1815 to consultation with Mr. Ferguson and the other partners 'of the new concern in Oxford Street' (letter in the Grosvenor Estate Archives kindly communicated by Mr. V. Belcher). The Gillow records show that Richard Gillow's three

sons were gradually withdrawing capital to about 1820.

3 Information in a letter from Companies House.

4 *A History of Gillow of Lancaster* (as note 1) p. 9 also gives as the earliest stamp GILLOWS
                        LANCASTER
In recent years other stamped marks have come to light, notably GILLOWS, which I take to be that used by the London manufactory.

5 The late Alex Lewis 'confessed' to me and, I understand, to Peter Thornton; other dealers have since confirmed that they did the same.

6 A 1797 advertisement for the auction of elegant furniture and effects of 'A Man of Fashion' at No. 24, Piccadilly with 'very excellent Cabinet Furniture of every description, by that excellent maker, Mr. GILLOW, of Oxford Street' is reproduced in Bertha Shaw, 'Gillows of Lancaster', *Country Life*, CII, 29 August 1947, p. 430; the Liverpool advertisements are in the Gillow files at the Department of Furniture, Victoria & Albert Museum.

7 'Die ersten Fabrikanten und Verkäufer in London sind Geo. und Rich. Gillow (P.A. Nemnich, *Neuste Reise durch England, Schottland, und Ireland* Tübingen, 1807, p. 136).

8 R.W. Symonds, 'A Suite of Dining Room Furniture' in *The Antique Collector*, Nov.–Dec. 1946; Sarah C. Nicholls, 'Furniture made by Gillow and Company for Workington Hall' in *Antiques*, CXXVII, no. 6, June 1985.

9 Nicholas Goodison, 'Gillows' Clock Cases' in *Antiquarian Horology*, V, no. 10, March 1968; Susan Stuart, 'The First White Dial Longcase Clocks and their Cases, 1772–1773' in *Antiquarian Horology*, XIII, no. 6, Dec. 1982; Id., '"A Neat Clockcase Ornamented" a 1760 Gillow drawing discovered', in Ibid., XV, no. 2, Dec. 1984.

10 Nicholas Goodison and John Hardy, 'Gillows at Tatton Park', in *Furniture History*, VI, 1970.

11 Sarah Nicholls, 'A Journey through the Gillow Records' in *Antique Collecting*, 20, no. 9, Feb. 1986.

12 Lindsay Boynton, 'Sir Roger Newdigate's Commodes' in *Antique Collecting*, 26, no. 2, June 1991.

13 Lindsay Boynton, 'Gillows' Furnishings for Catholic Chapels 1750–1800' in *Studies in Church History*, 28, 1992.

14 K.E. Ingram, 'Furniture and the Plantation: Further Light on the West Indian Trade of an English Furniture Firm in the Eighteenth Century', in *Furniture History*, XXVIII, 1992.

15 Percy Macquoid, *A History of English Furniture, IV, The Age of Satinwood 1770–1820* (1908, reprinted by Dover, 1972), p. 148.

16 Charles F. Montgomery, *American Furniture of the Federal Period* (New York, 1966), p. 15.

17 By Clive Wainwright in *Pugin. A Gothic Passion*, ed. Paul Atterbury and Clive Wainwright (New Haven and London 1994), p. 127.

18 The edition used here is by Charles F. Montgomery and Wilfred P. Cole, with an Introduction by Lindsay O.J. Boynton, (Praeger Publishers Inc., New York, 1970).

19 Peter Ward-Jackson, *English Furniture Designs of the Eighteenth Century* (1958), pp. 25–6, 61–6. The edition of the *Guide* used here is the reprint by Dover (New York, 1969) of the 3rd edn.

20 Neil McKendrick, John Brewer, and J.H. Plumb, *The Birth of a Consumer Society* (1983), p. 28.

21 My calculation from the Waste Books.

22 Westminster City Archives (hereafter WCA) 344/175/42: letter dated 27.3.1801.

23 The alcove bed and the curtains of Colour Plates 19, 20 appear to be after Sheraton, although the Gillow designs are undated; examples of Sheraton borrowing from Gillow are the corner night table dated 1793 (*Drawing-Book*, Appendix, Plate 23 at p. 44, right-hand. This is essentiallly the night table made by Gillows in 1789 (see Fig. 102), although this had a straight back. The chair in Fig. 280 dated 1792 is the basis of Sheraton's undated version in the *Drawing-Book*'s Appendix, Plate 6 at p. 12. (left-hand).

24 See Figs. 124–5.

25 Ward-Jackson, *English Furniture Designs*, p. 66; Sheraton, *Drawing-Book*, pp. 353, 417.

26 WCA, 344/90/13.

27 See my forthcoming book on *Gillow Furniture*. For the present by far the best account, though not entirely accurate, is Ivan Hall's entry in the *Dictionary of English Furniture-Makers 1660–1840*, ed. Geoffrey Beard and Christopher Gilbert (1986).

28 The first extant records in the Gillow Archive date from 1731 (WCA 344/1).

29 Cf. *The Autobiography of William Stout of Lancaster, 1665–1752*, ed. J.D. Marshall, (Chetham Society, Manchester, 1967), p. 59.

30 Both I and Paul Harrison have come independently to this conclusion. I am indebted to Paul Harrison for kindly showing me his undergraduate dissertation on Gillows.

31 Robert in 1785, George in 1787, Richard in 1796.

32 WCA 344/735/2. But see the introductory

remarks in the Notes to the Colour plates, where the suggestion is made that some plates may be the work of the London branch.

33 J.M. Robinson, *Samuel Wyatt, Architect*, (unpublished Oxford D. Phil. thesis), *passim*. At present there is little guidance available on Wyatt furniture apart from Frances Fergusson, 'Wyatt Chairs: Rethinking the Adam Heritage' in *The Burlington Magazine*, CXIX, July 1977. John Cornforth informs me that his articles on Wyatt ornament await publication in *Country Life*. Among the illustrations in the present book I take the following to be Wyatt features: vases (Colour Plates 21, 23), rams' heads (Colour Plate 22), small vases in the frieze of sideboards (Fig. 85) and the tablets in sideboards (Figs. 89–91, 95, 97). Among many such features in the section on girandoles and pier glasses are vases (Figs. 204, 211) and tripods (Figs. 211–2; cf. 217).

34 Cf. Eileen Harris, *The Furniture of Robert Adam* (1963), *passim*, especially plates 7–12, 14–15, 17, 23–4, 26, 28–30, 37–47.

35 Montgomery, *American Furniture*, (as note 16), p. 15.

36 Simon Jervis, 'Holland and Sons, and the Furnishing of the Athenaeum' in *Furniture History*, VI, 1970, 43.

37 Variously called waste books, day books, journals.

38 As estimated by Goodison and Hardy (as note 10), p. 1.

39 WCA 344/93–98.

40 WCA 344/89–90.

41 WCA 344/67.

42 WCA 735/1: a selection from this volume was published by Ivan Hall, 'Patterns of elegance: the Gillows' furniture designs', in *Country Life*, 8 June 1978, pp. 1612–15, and 'Models with a choice of leg' 15 June, 1978, pp. 1740–2.

43 Codified in 1785, but Gillows' correspondence shows that it was effective from 1783.

44 Especially Christopher Hussey, *English Country Houses: Late Georgian, 1800–1840* (1958), pp. 91–102.

45 Samuel and Lewis William.

46 See note 10.

47 See note 13.

48 Coffins were excluded from the Estimate Sketch Books after 1787.

49 Illustrated in Christopher Gilbert, *Back-Stairs Furniture* (exhibition catalogue, Temple Newsam House, Leeds, 1977), no. 21.

50 Illustrated in Ibid., no. 25.

51 Illustrated in Ibid., no. 28.

52 Cf. Roy Porter, *Health for Sale. Quacking in England 1660–1850* (Manchester, 1989), esp. pp. 36–9, 42–3 on self-dosing, and contemporary works such as *Every Man His Own Physician* (1766).

53 WCA 344/89/10.

54 Cf. Christopher Gilbert, 'London and Provincial Books of Prices: Comment and Bibliography' in *Furniture History*, XVIII, 1982, 15 where the term is defined as 'the facade of letter holes, small drawers, etc.' in a sliding secretary drawer; but the contemporary description as 'A sliding prospect, the pilaster drawer to take out behind' (Ibid., p. 23), and Gillows' references always indicate a sliding till rather than a facade; furthermore the term was applied where there was no sliding secretary drawer, e.g. in a desk (i.e. in modern terms a bureau with sloping front).

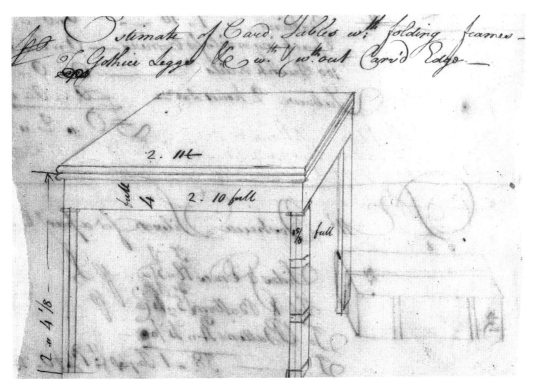

1 Card table with gothic legs, 1762.

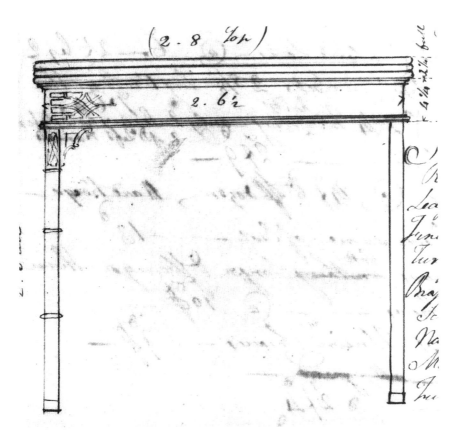

2 Universal table with gothic legs, 1761.

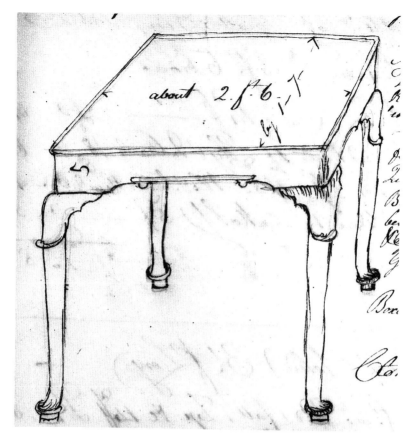

about 2.f.6. 1.T.

3   Universal table, 1760.

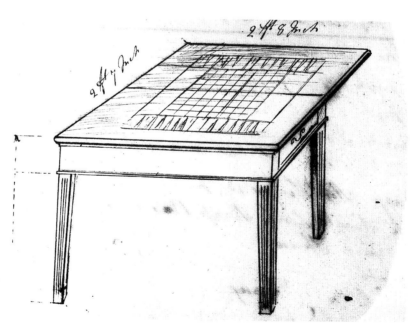

4   Universal table, 1787.

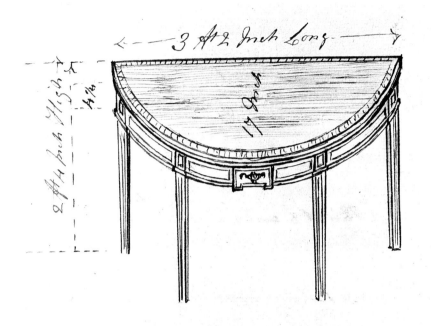

5   Card table, 1787.

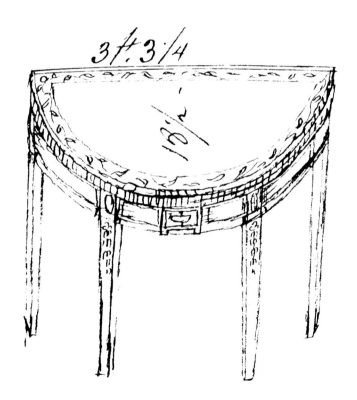

6   Card table, 1787.

7　Card table, 1794.

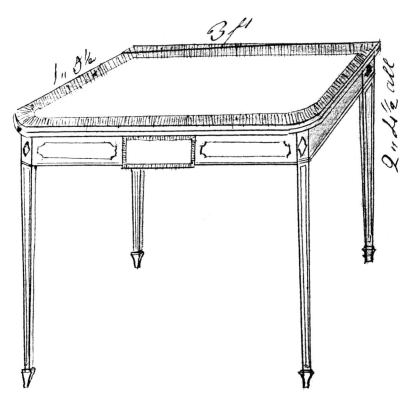

8　Card table, 1797.

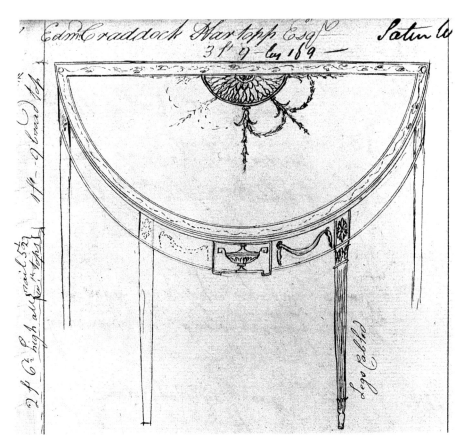

9   Inlaid card table, 1784.

10   Painted pier table, 1793.

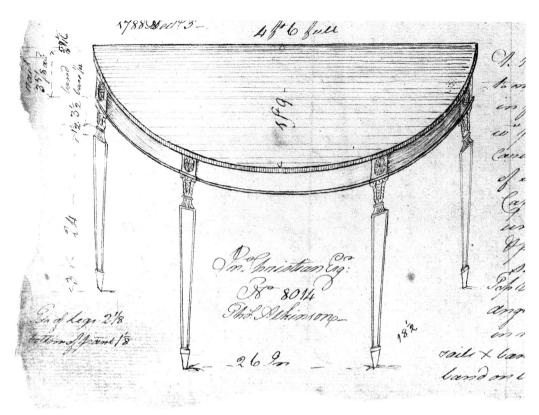

11 Pier table, 1788.

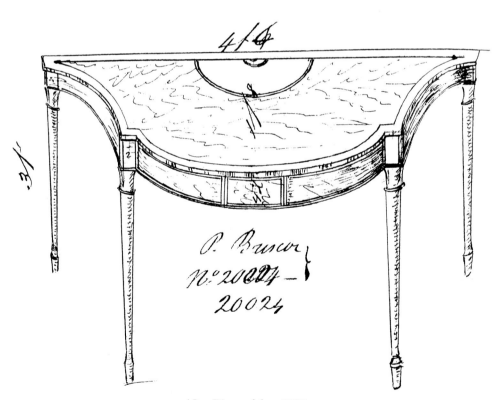

12 Pier table, 1793.

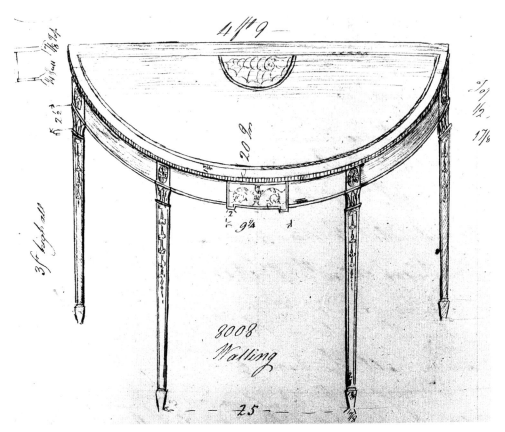

13   Pier table with inlaid shell, 1788.

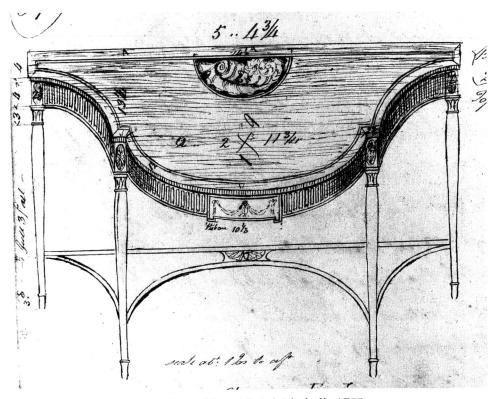

14   Pier table with inlaid shell, 1788.

15   Pier table, 1790.

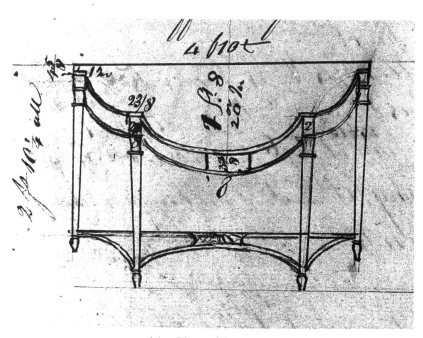

16   Pier table, 1789.

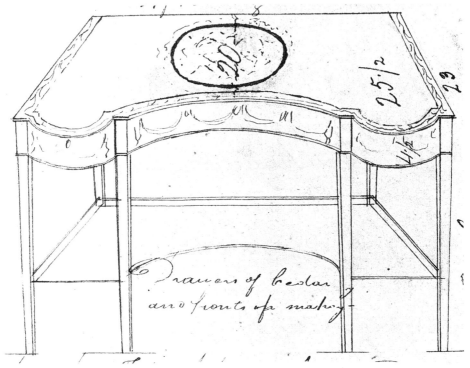

17 Pier table, 1795.

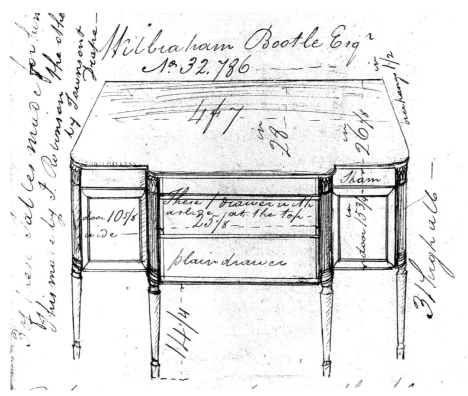

18 Pier table or commode, 1795.

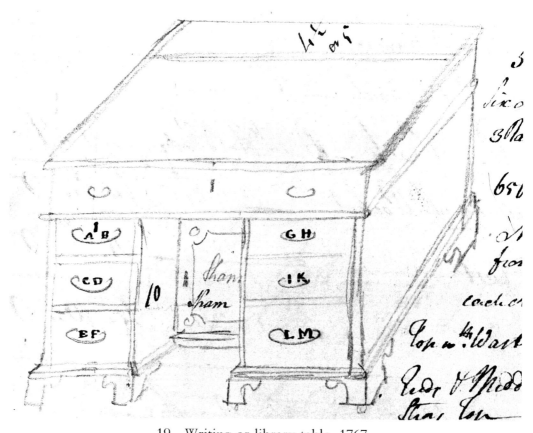

19   Writing or library table, 1767.

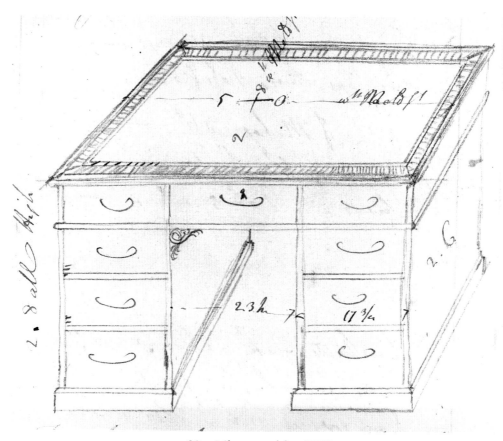

20   Library table, 1768.

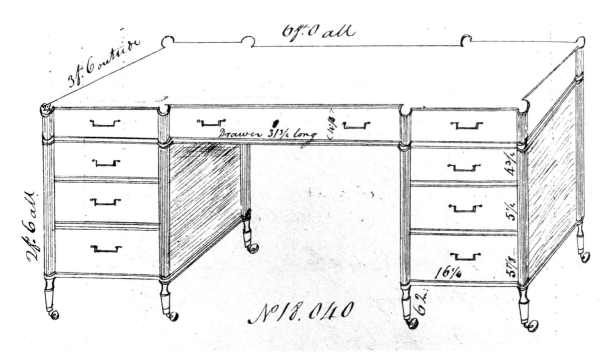

6ft. 0 all

3 ft. Outside

2 ft. 6 all

Drawer 31¾ long

14⅜

4¾
5¼
5⅝
16¼
6 2

No 18.040

21   Library table, 1792.

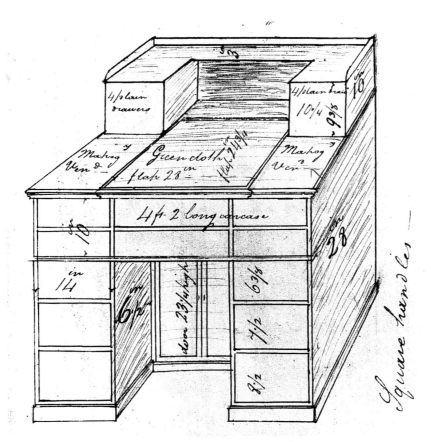

4/plain drawers

4/plain drawers

in 10

10¼ 9⅝

Mahog
Ven.d

Green cloth
flap 28 —— in

flap 21¾

Mahog
Ven.d

in 10

in 28

4 ft. 2 long carcase

in 14

6in

door 23¾ high

6¾

7½

8½

Square handles —

22   Bureau and bookshelf, 1795.

23 Writing-table, 1787.

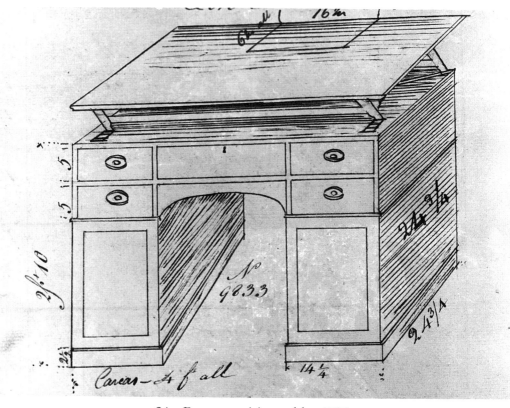

24 Bureau writing-table, 1789.

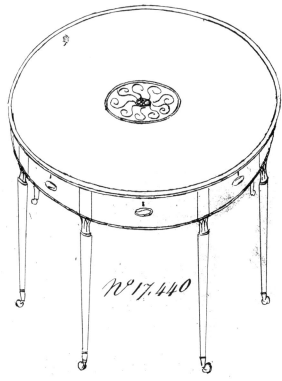

25　Library table, 1789.

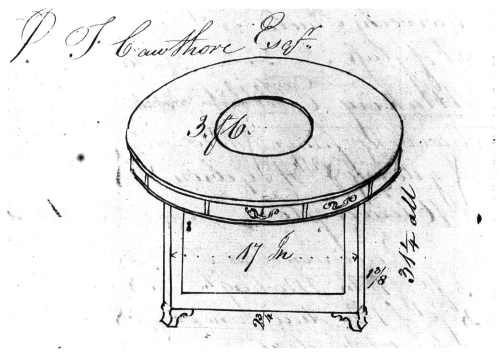

26　Library table, 1792.

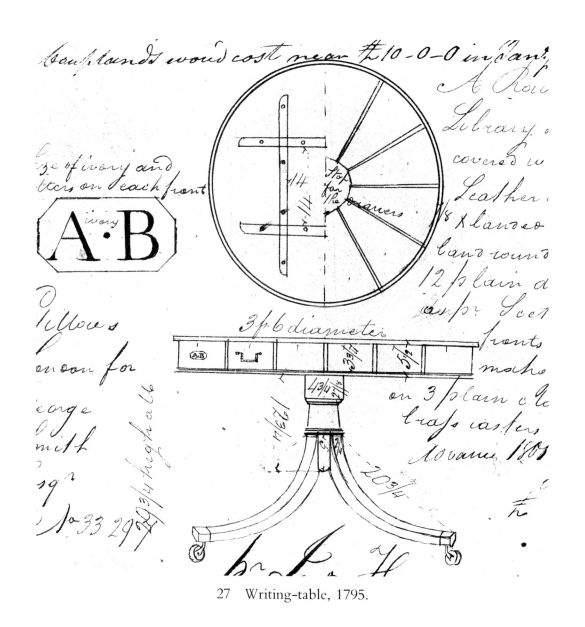

27 Writing-table, 1795.

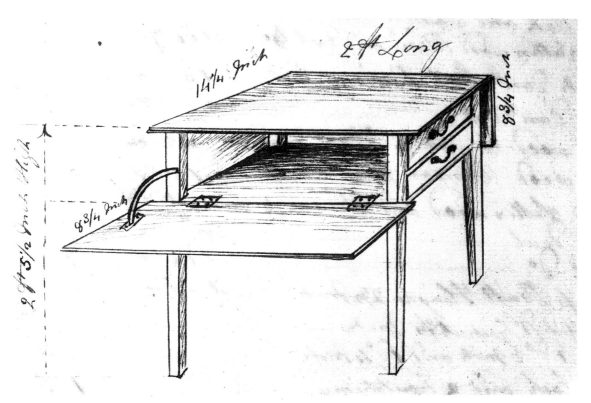

28 Deception table, 1787.

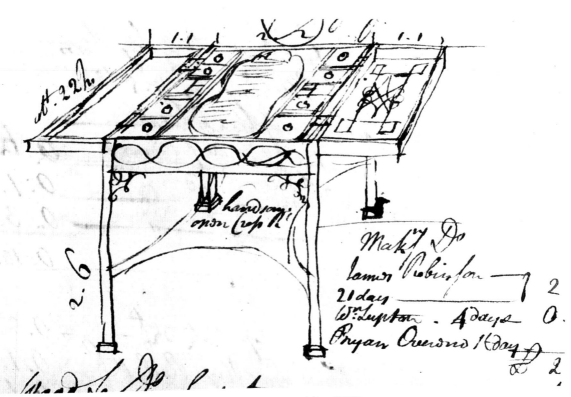

29 Dressing-table, 1770.

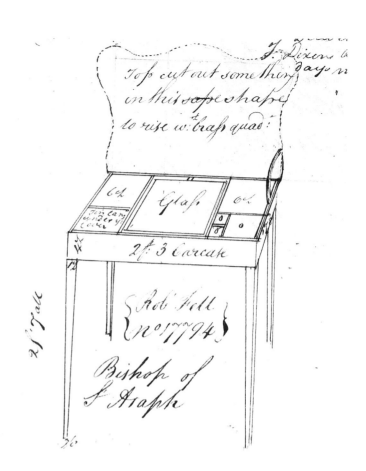

30 Dressing-table, 1792.

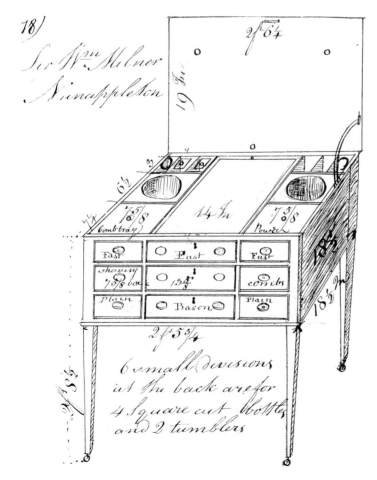

31 Dressing-table, 1789.

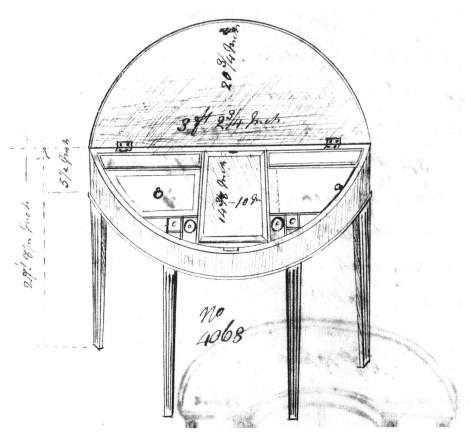

32 Lady's dressing-table, 1787.

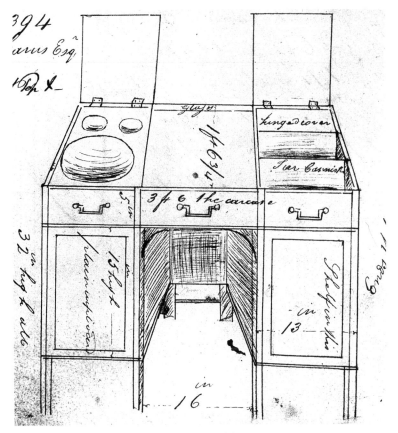

33 Dressing-table, 1794.

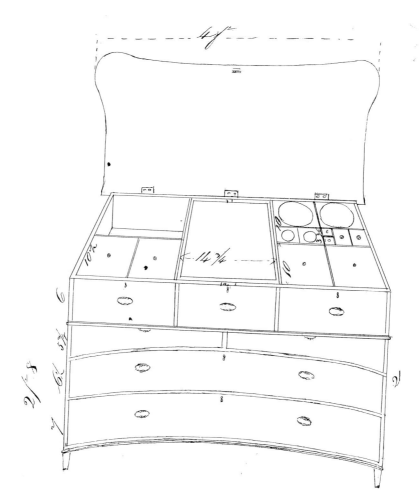

34 Dressing-table, 1791.

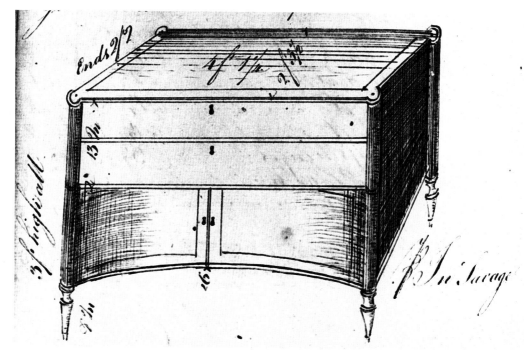

35 Writing-table, 1790.

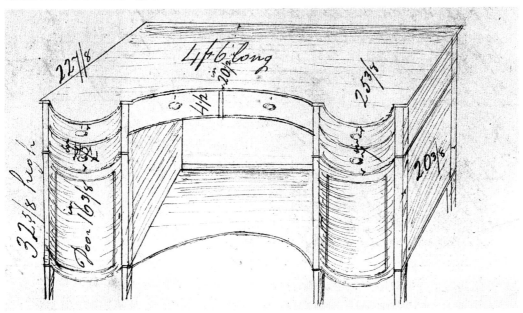

J. Unsworth Esqr
No 12819

Tops overhang
2½ in front
over ends 2 in
at back 1¾ in

The right hand door with
plain divisions
One side of the cupboard plain the other
with a loose shelf, upright partition

36   Dressing-table, 1790.

37   Dressing-table, about 1790.

38   Dressing or pier table, 1795.

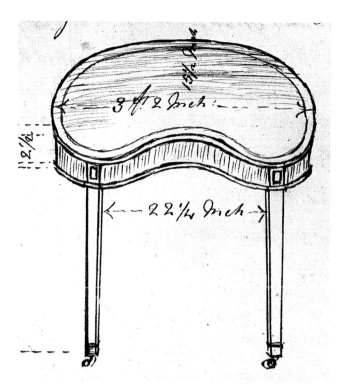

39 Writing-table, 1787.

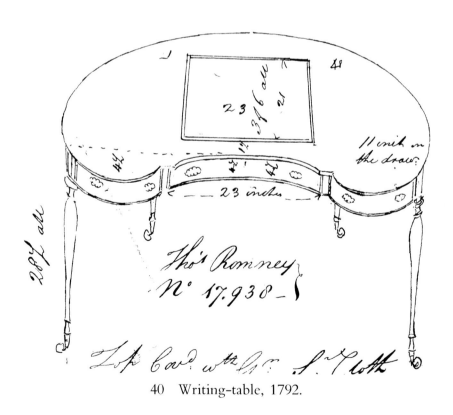

40 Writing-table, 1792.

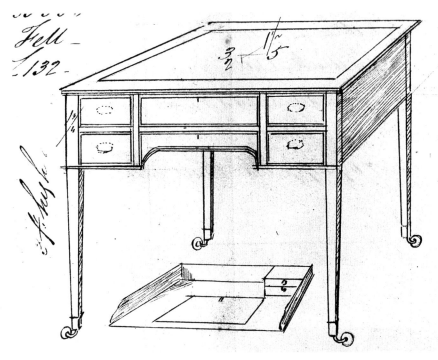

41   Writing-table, 1794.

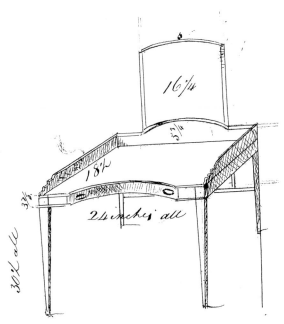

42   Harlequin writing-table, 1791.

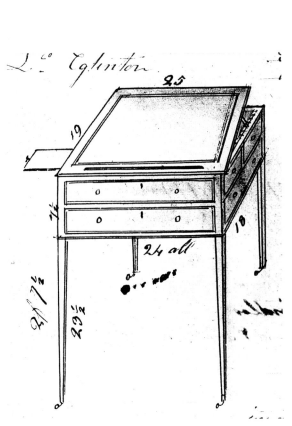

43   'Watson's' writing-table, 1799.

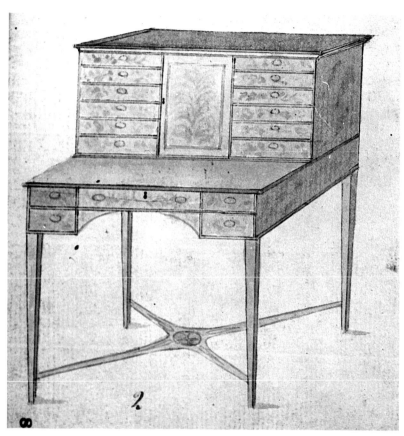

44 Writing-table with cupboard, about 1790/95.

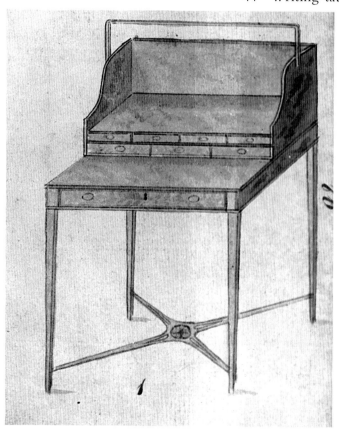

45 Writing-table and bookshelf, about 1790/95.

46 Writing-table, 1795.

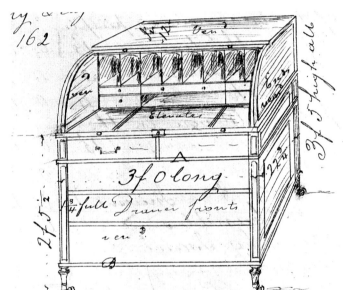

47 Writing-desk, 1796.

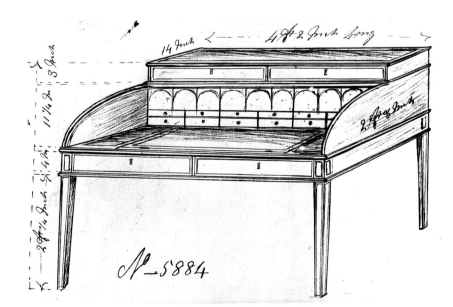

48 Writing-table, 1787.

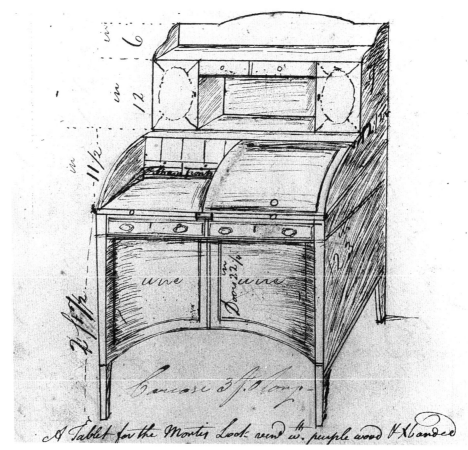

A Tablet for the Monti Lock reed w. purple wood & X banded

49 Writing-desk, 1794.

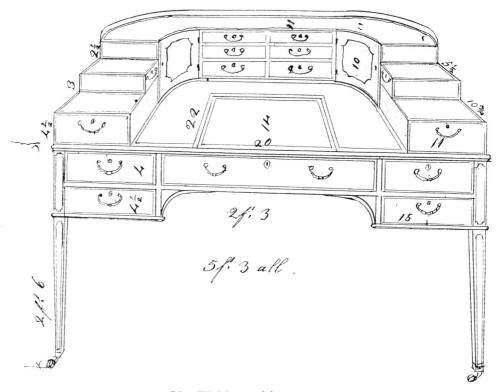

50 Writing-table, 1798.

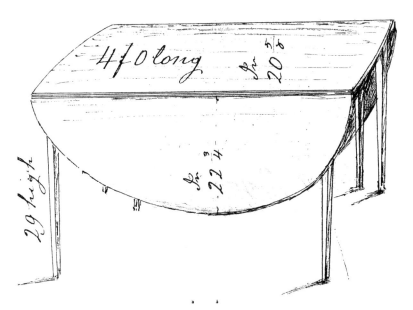

4f 0 long

In 20 5/8

29 high

In 22 3/4

51   Oval dining-table, 1796.

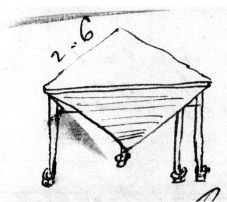

2:6

52   Corner table, 1768 or 1769.

136

Swelno 10 in

4ft 6 long

Ft 3 in

A mahogany break
fast Table top ven.ᵈ
on mahogany astragal
edge molding Ander the top
rails ven on oalᵗ astragal
round bottom of rails fluted
legs Joint in the top —

29 in high

53   Breakfast table, 1794.

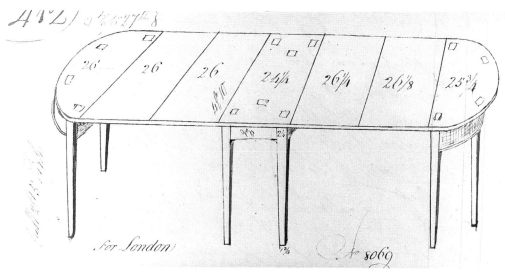

54 Set of dining-tables, 1788.

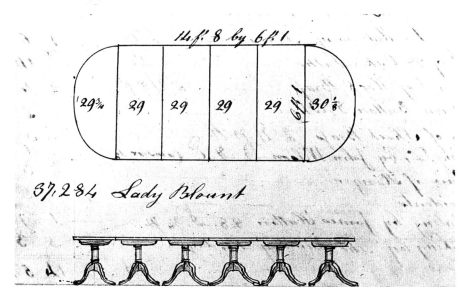

55 Set of dining-tables, 1798.

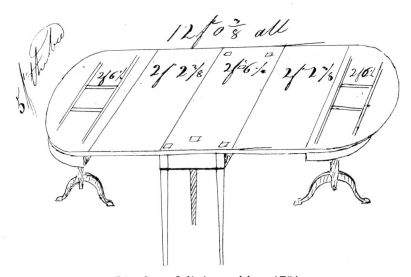

56 Set of dining-tables, 1791

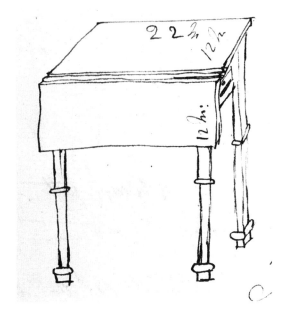

57   Small table, 1766.

58   'Fly' table, 1770.

59   Pembroke table, 1772.

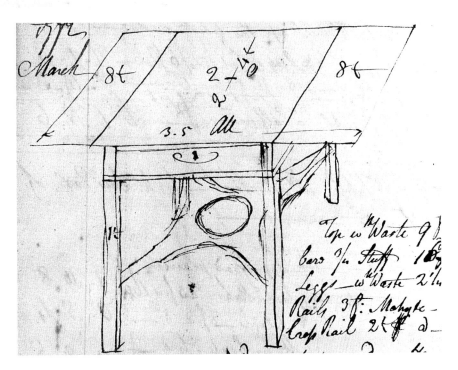

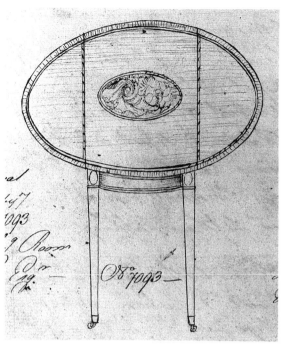

60   Pembroke table, 1788.

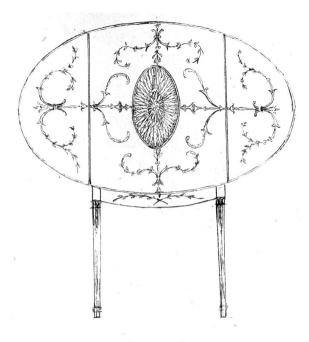

61   Pembroke table, 1784.

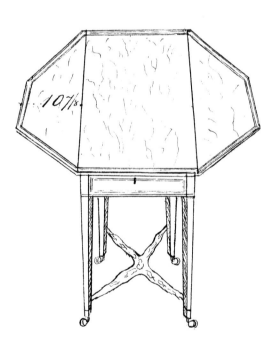

62   Octagonal pembroke table, 1794.

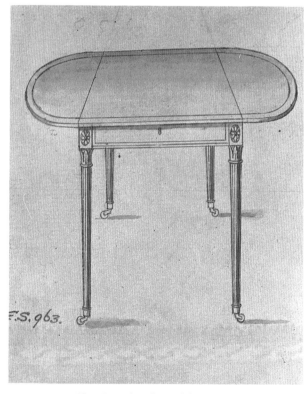

63   Pembroke table, 1793.

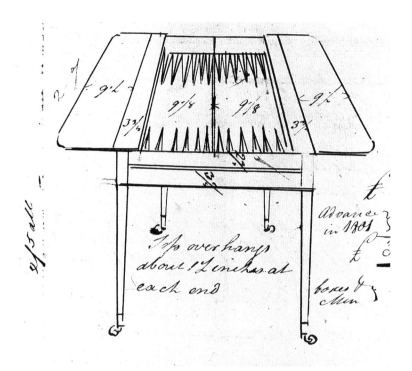

64   Pembroke games table, 1793.

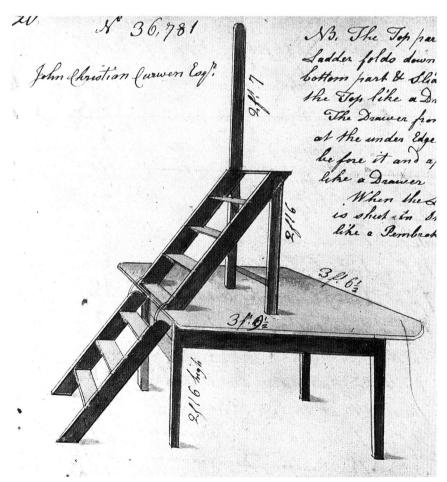

65   Pembroke table and library ladder, 1798.

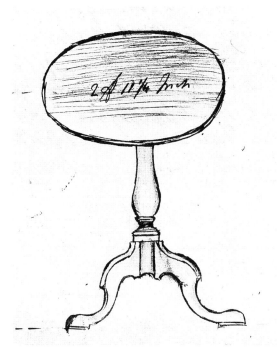

66   Snap table, 1787.

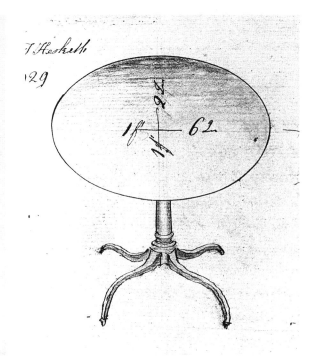

67   Work table, 1798.

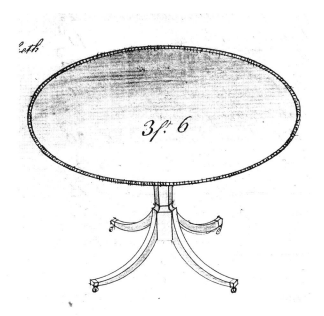

68   Snap table, 1798.

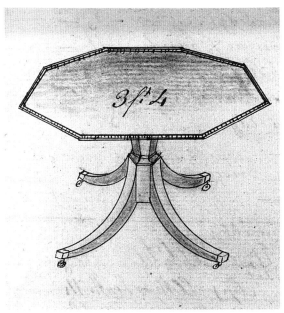

69   Octagonal snap table, 1798.

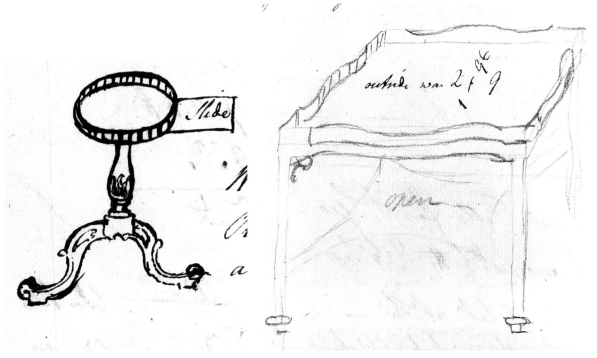

70   Tea kettle stand, 1769.

71   Tea table, 1767.

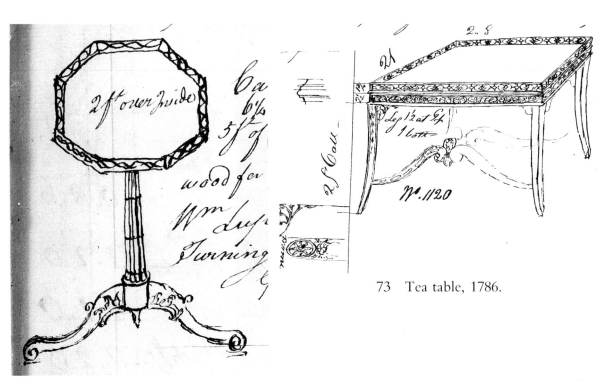

73   Tea table, 1786.

72   Tea table, 1767.

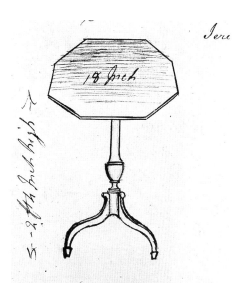

74 Work table, 1788.

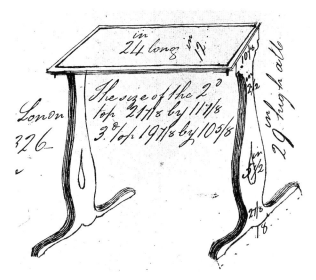

75 Work table, 1795.

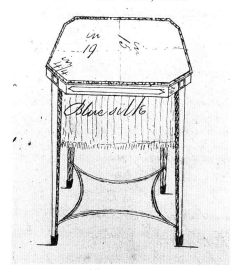

76 Work table, 1794.

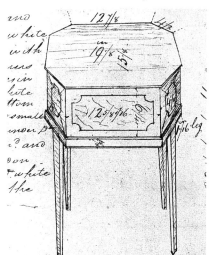

77 Work table, 1795.

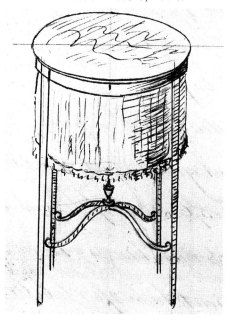

78 Work table, 1793.

79 Frame for a marble top, 1795.

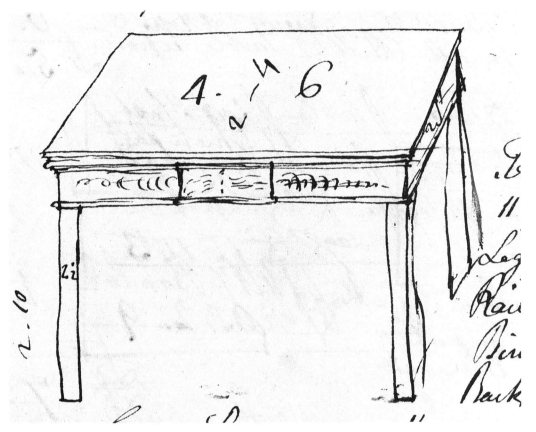

80   Sideboard table, 1771.

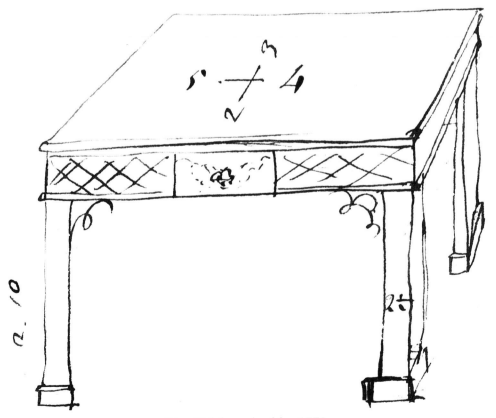

81   Sideboard table, 1770.

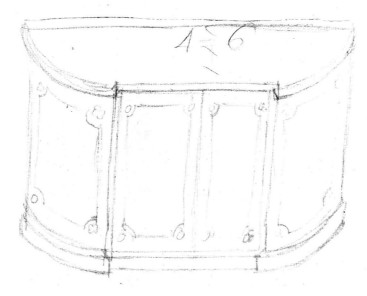

82   Plate case, 1767.

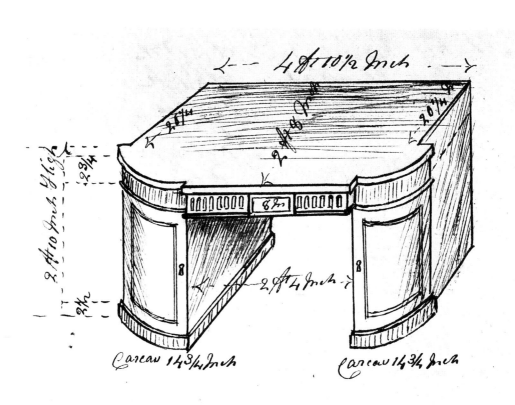

83   Sideboard table, 1787.

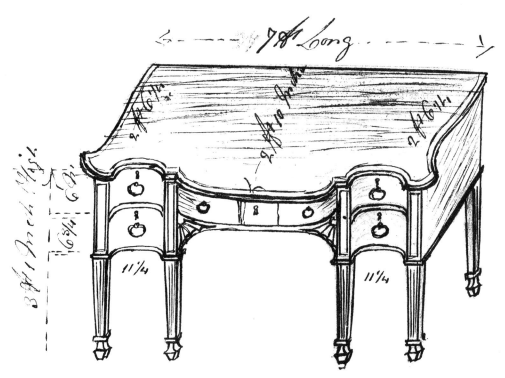

84   Sideboard table, 1787.

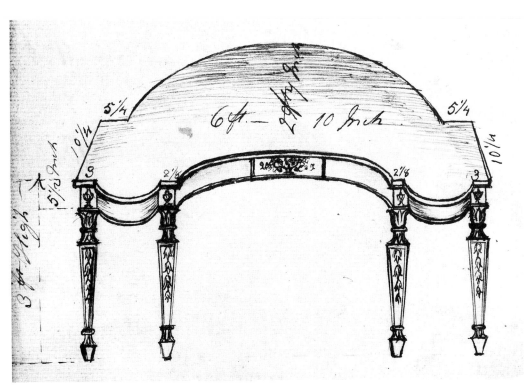

85   Sideboard table, 1787.

86 Sideboard table, 1794.

87 Sideboard table, 1787.

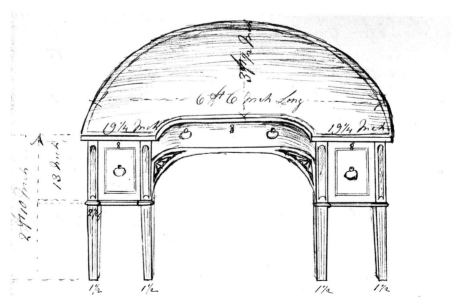

88 Sideboard table, 1787.

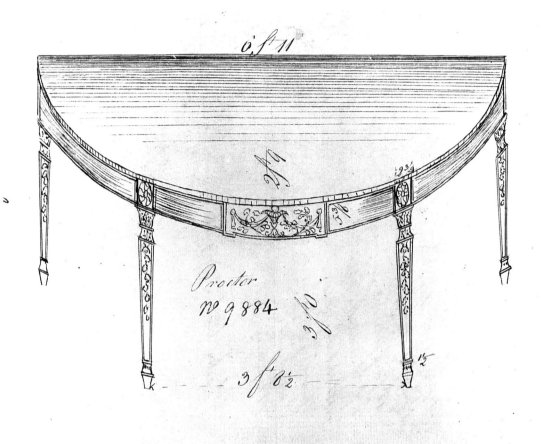

89   Sideboard table, 1789.

90   Sideboard table, 1788.

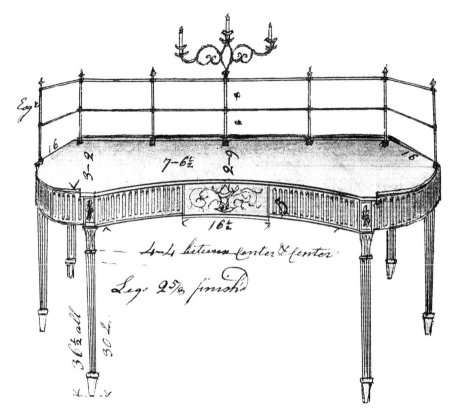

91 Sideboard table, 1797.

92 Sideboard table, 1799.

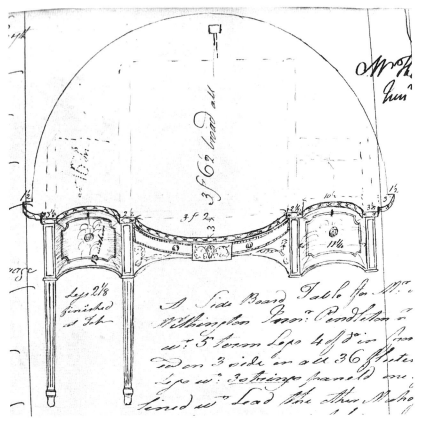

93   Sideboard table, 1786.

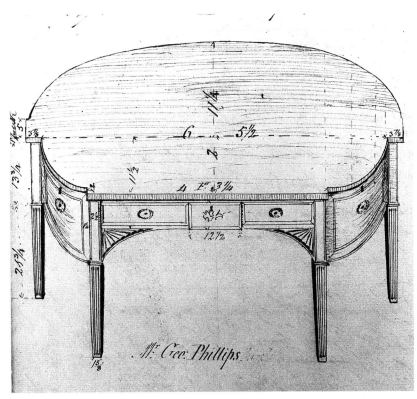

94   Sideboard table, 1788.

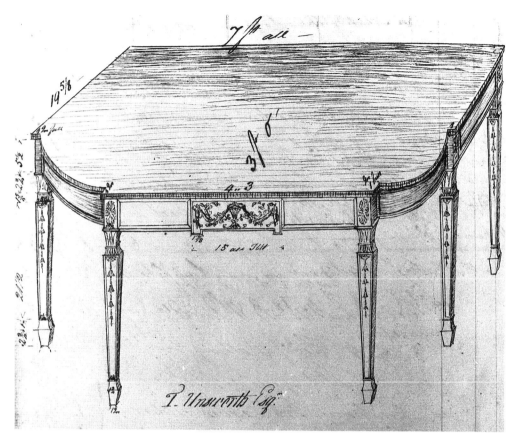

95   Sideboard table, 1788.

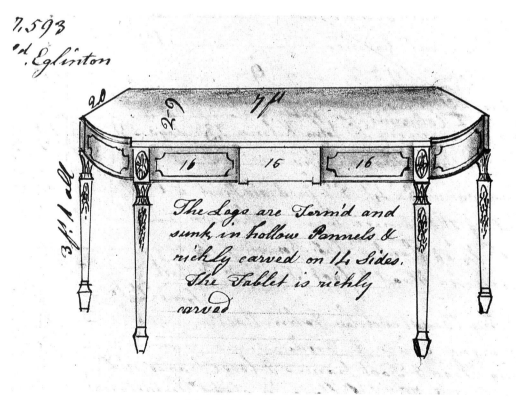

96   Sideboard table, 1799.

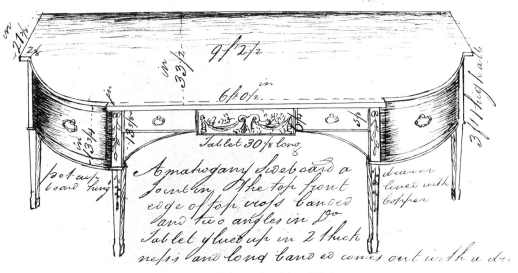

A mahogany Sideboard a
Sembley. The top front
edge of top cross banded
and two angles in Do
Tablet glued up in 2 thick
ness, and long band ed comes out with a de

97   Sideboard table, 1794.

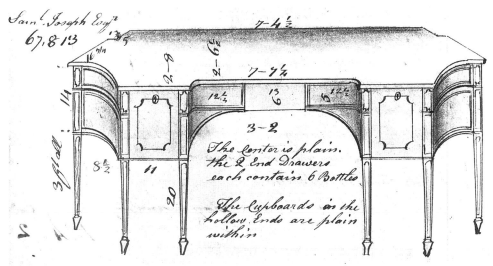

Saml. Joseph Esqr.
67, 8 13

The Center is plain,
the 2 End Drawers
each contain 6 Bottles

The Cupboards in the
hollow Ends are plain
within

98   Sideboard table, 1799.

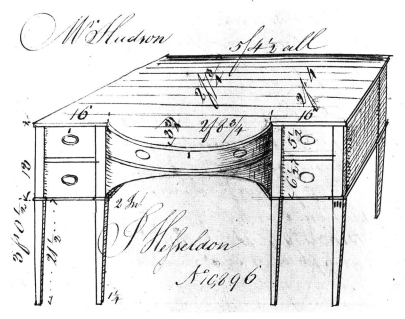

Mr Hudson

R Wheeldon
No 1096

99   Sideboard table, 1789.

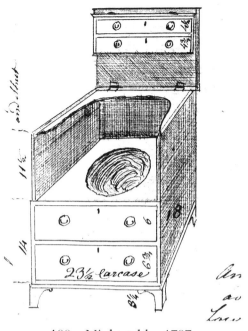

100   Night table, 1797.

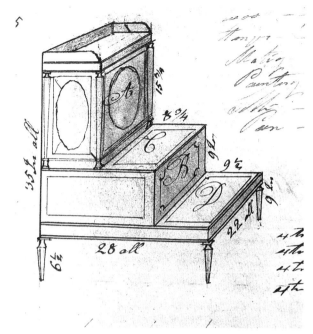

101   Night table, 1799.

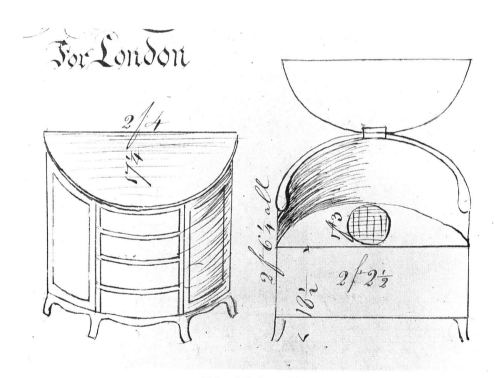

102   Night table, 1789.

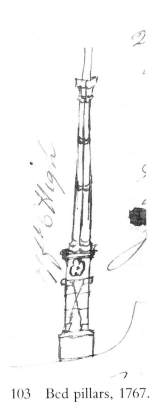

103   Bed pillars, 1767.

104   Bedstead, 1788.

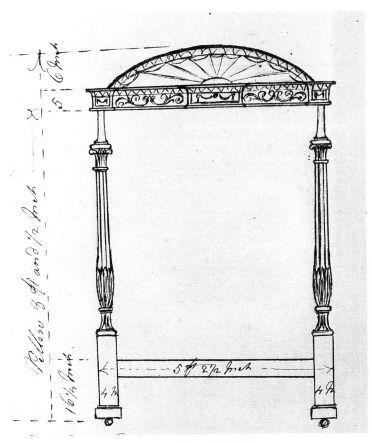

105   Bedstead, 1788.

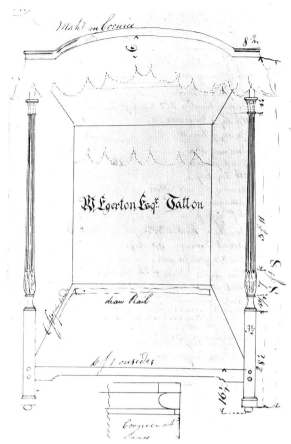

106   Bedstead, 1789.

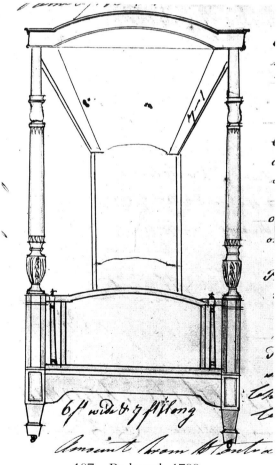

107   Bedstead, 1799.

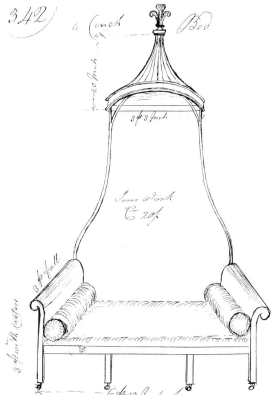

108 Couch bed, 1788.

109 Couch bed, about 1790.

110   Press-bed, 1771.

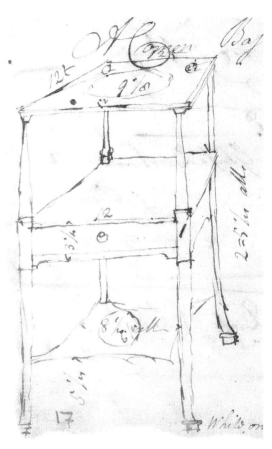

111   Bason stand, 1760.

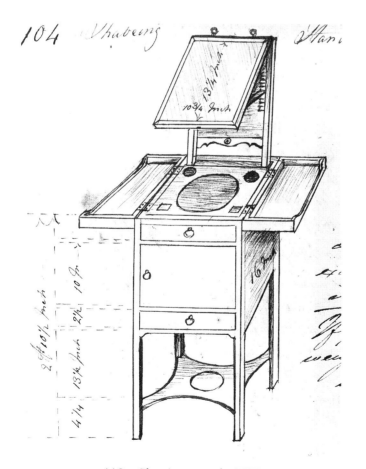

112   Shaving stand, 1787.

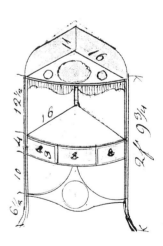

113   Corner washing stand, 1797.

114   Chest of drawers, 1787.

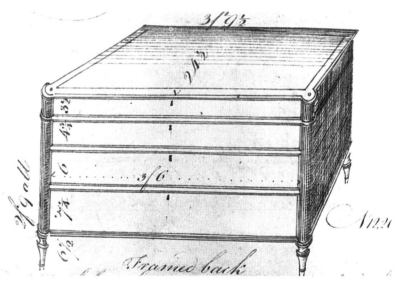

115   Chest of drawers, 1789.

116   Commode with toilet, 1799.

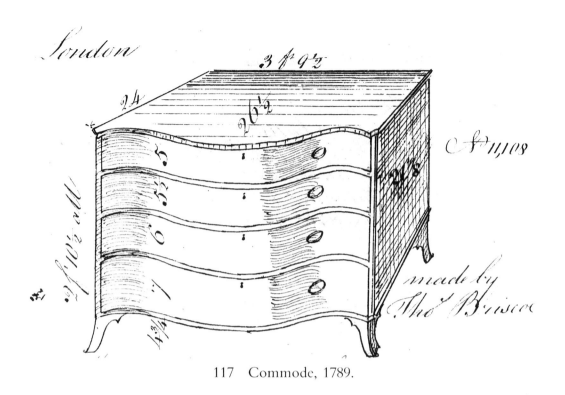

117   Commode, 1789.

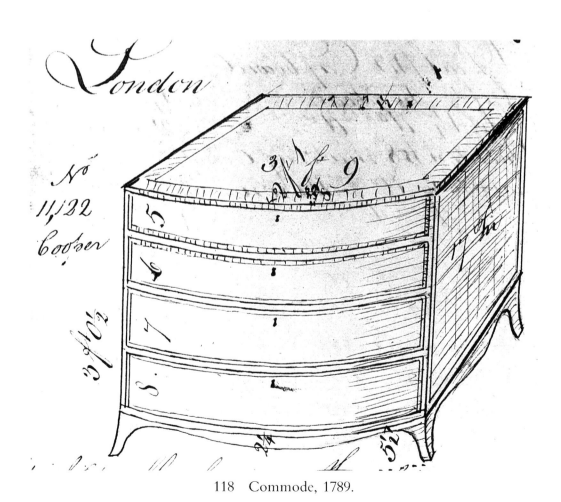

118   Commode, 1789.

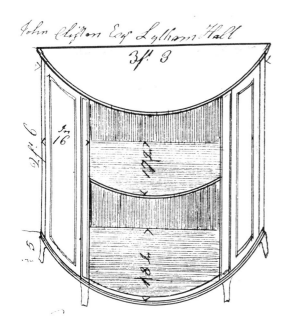

119 Commode, 1797.

120 Commode, 1787.

121 Commode, 1788.

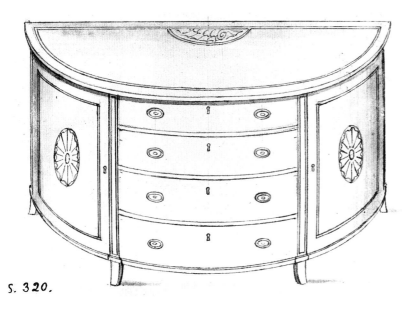

S. 320.

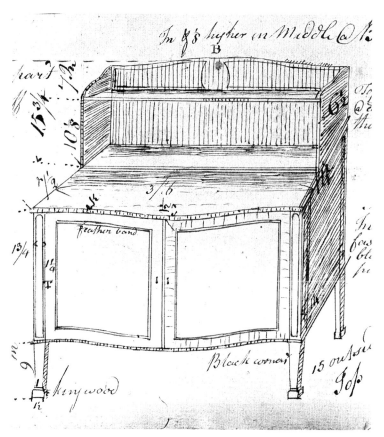

122   Commode, 1789.

123   Commode, 1790.

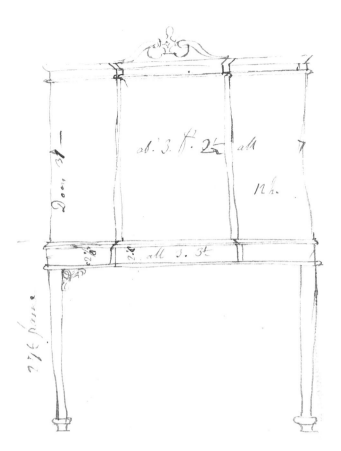

124 Cabinet, 1768.

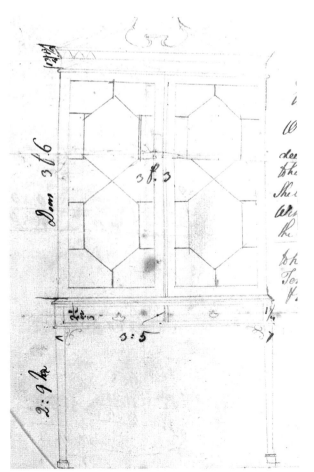

125 Plate case, 1770.

126   Cabinet, 1788.

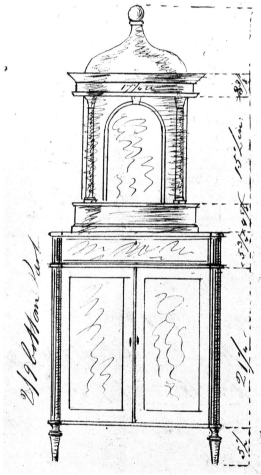

127   Cabinet, 1793.

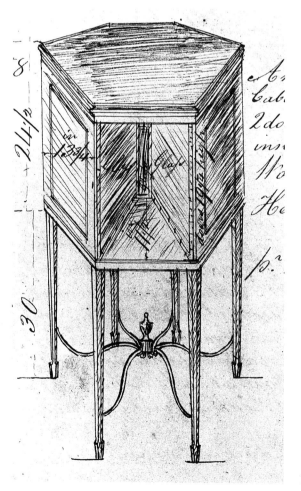

128   Cabinet, 1795.

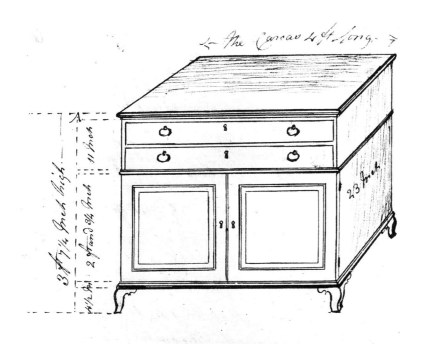

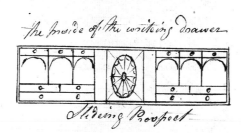

129   Low wardrobe with writing-drawer, 1788.

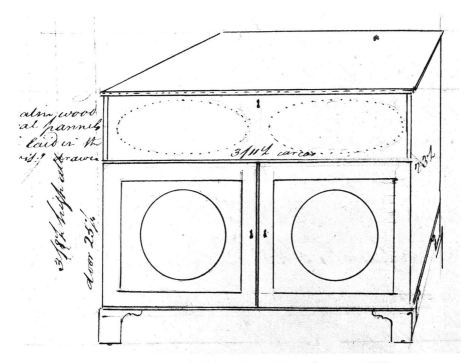

130   Low wardrobe with writing-drawer, 1793.

131   Clothes press, 1759.

132   Cabinet or bureau-wardrobe, 1788.

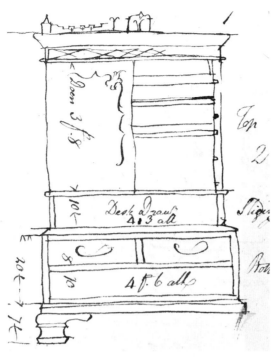

133 'A large piece of furniture', 1766.

134 Secretary and bookcase, 1787.

135   Wardrobe with writing-drawer, 1788.

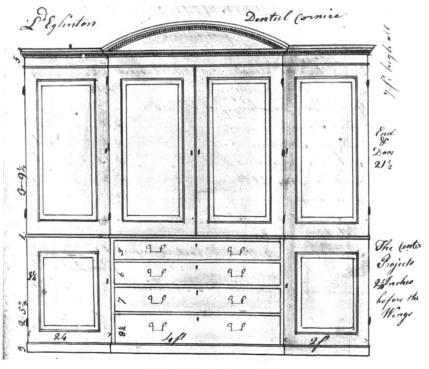

136   Wardrobe, 1799.

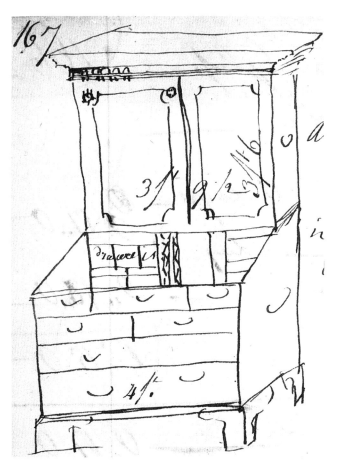

137 Desk and bookcase, 1771.

138 Bureau and bookcase, 1771.

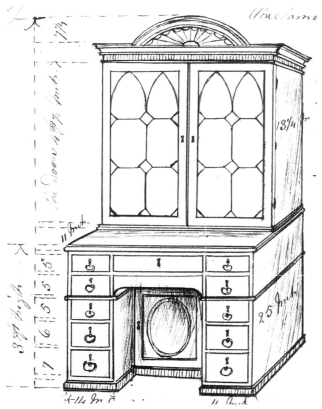

139 Bureau and bookcase, 1788.

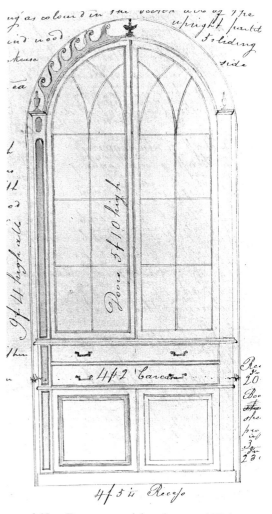

140 Bureau and bookcase, 1796.

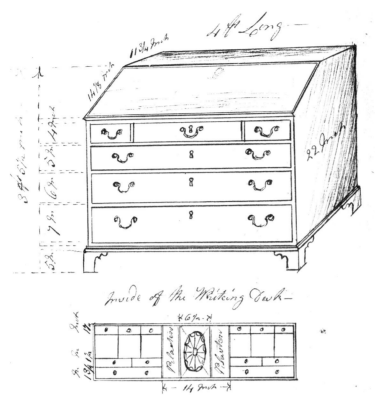

141   Writing-desk, 1787.

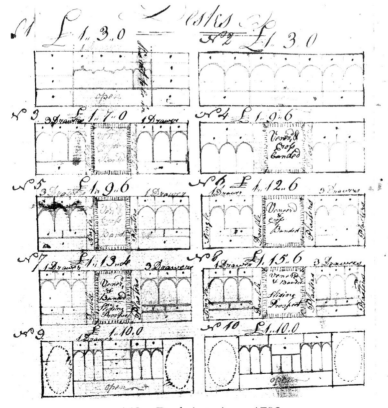

142   Desk interiors, 1792.

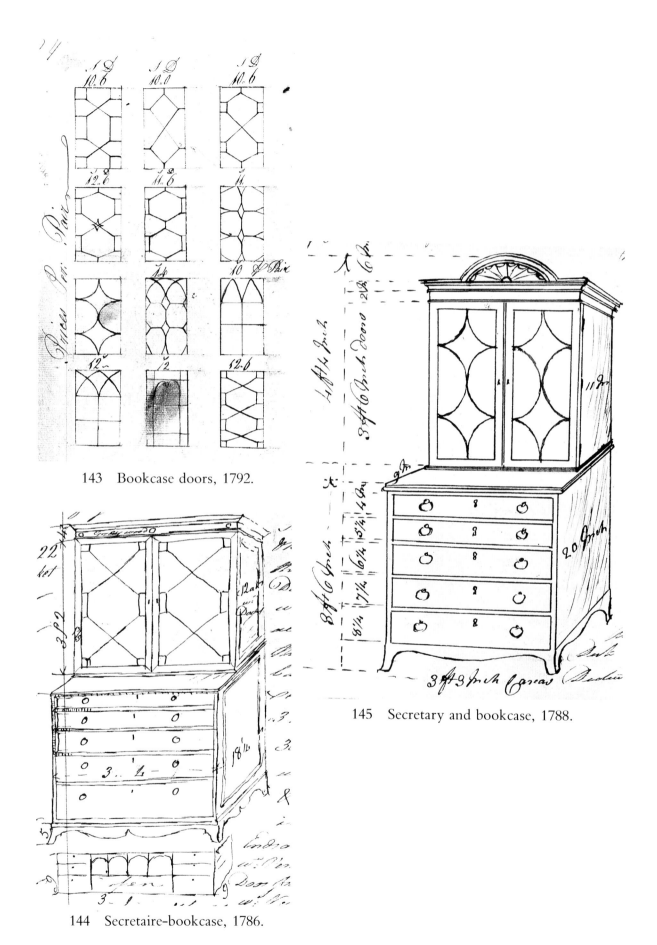

143   Bookcase doors, 1792.

144   Secretaire-bookcase, 1786.

145   Secretary and bookcase, 1788.

146   Secretaire, 1794.

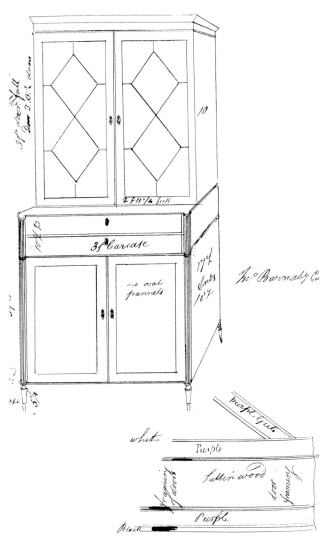

147   Secretaire and bookcase, 1792.

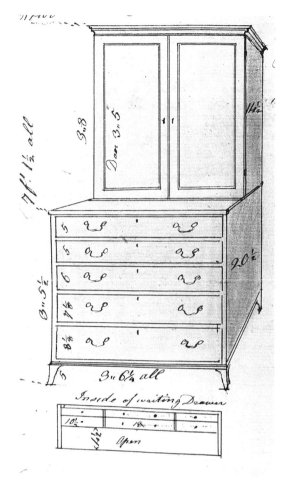

148   Secretaire and bookcase, 1797.

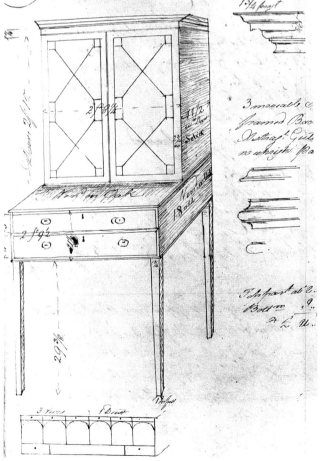

149   Secretaire on legs, 1788.

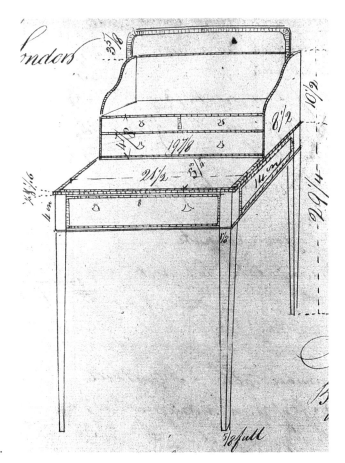

150 Sheveret, 1790.

151 Writing-table and bookshelf, 1796.

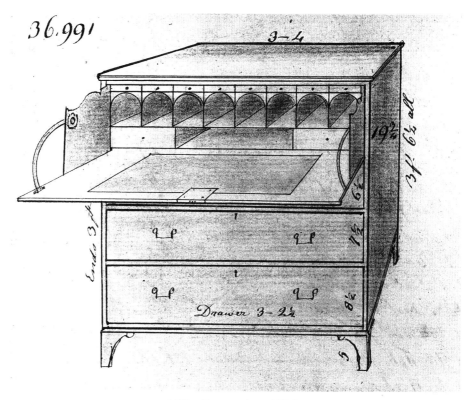

152   Secretaire, 1798.

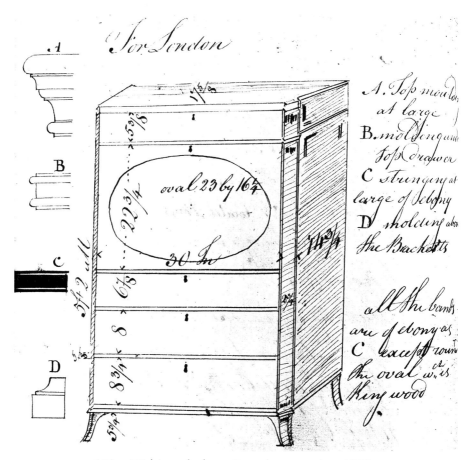

153   Writing-desk or French secretaire, 1789.

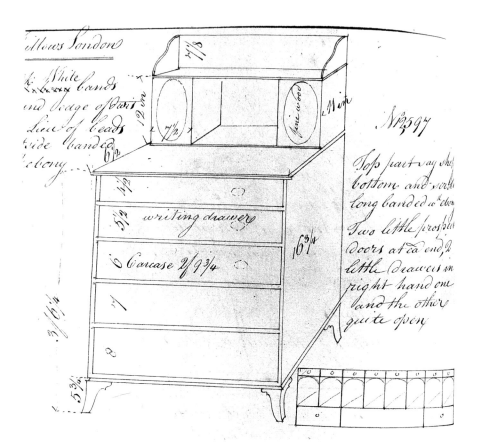

154 Secretaire and little bookcase, 1790.

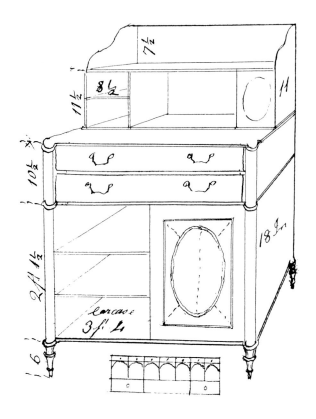

155 Secretaire and bookshelf, 1798.

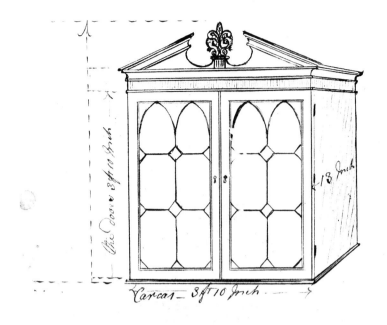

156 Bookcase, 1788.

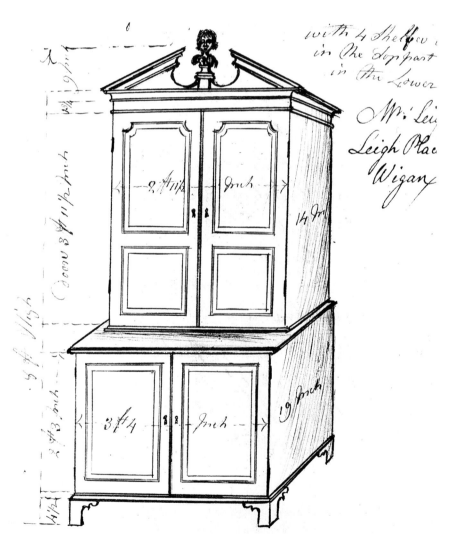

157 Bookcase, 1788.

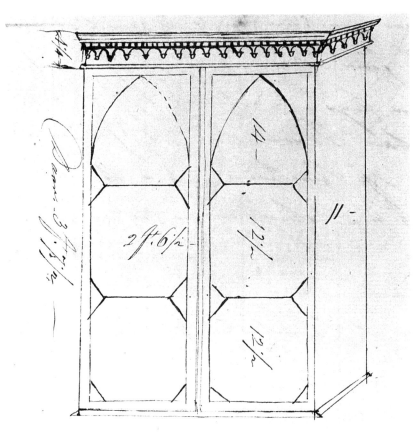

158   Bookcase, 1790.

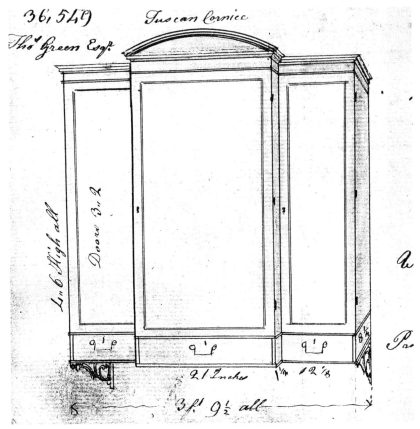

159   Hanging bookcase, 1797.

160   Bookshelf with drawers, 1788.

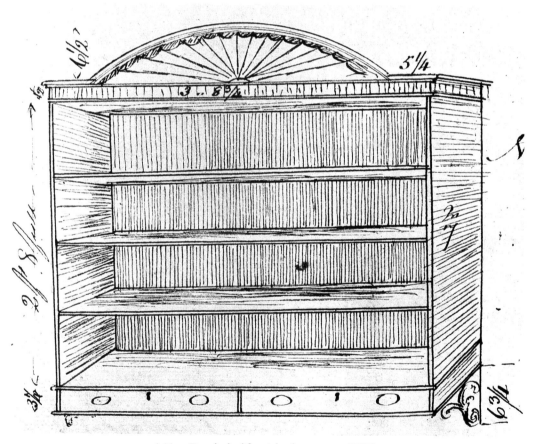

161   Bookshelf with drawers, 1788.

162 'Moving library', 1794.

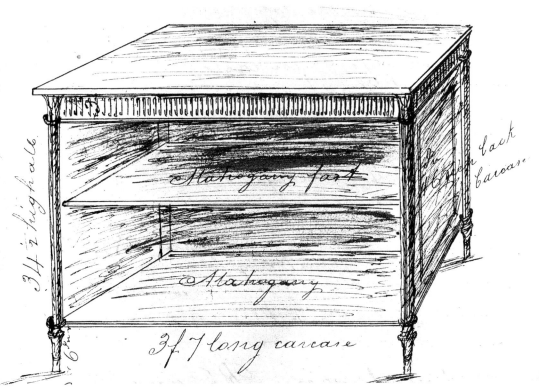

163 Frame for a marble slab, 1796.

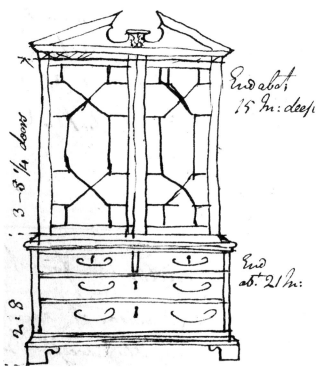

164   Small library bookcase, 1766.

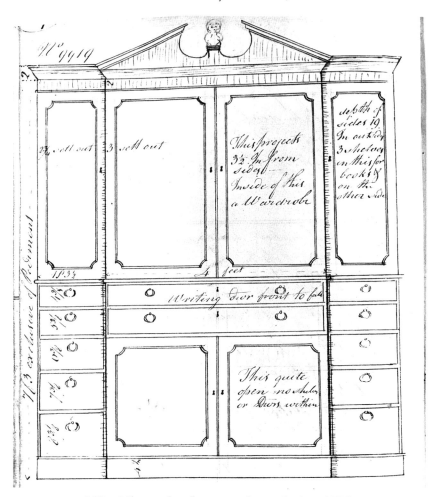

165   Library bookcase and wardrobe, 1789.

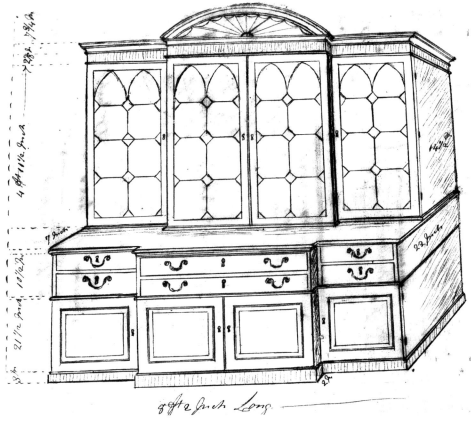

166 Library bookcase, 1787.

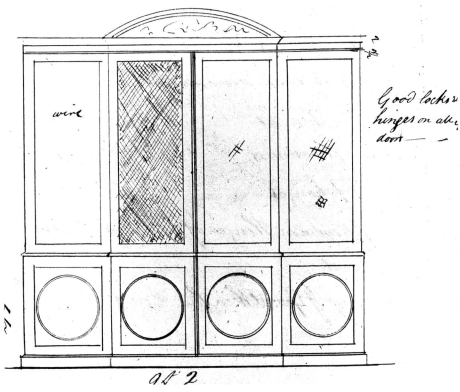

*Good locks &
hinges on all
doors*

wire

167 Library bookcase, 1792.

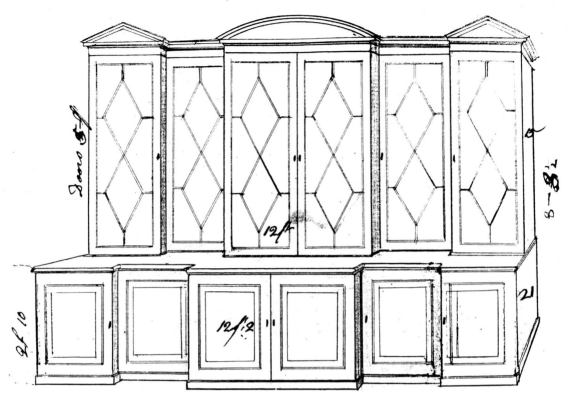

168   Library bookcase, 1797.

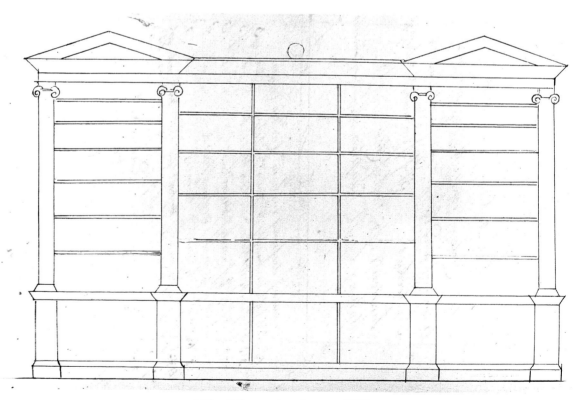

169   Library bookcase, 1792.

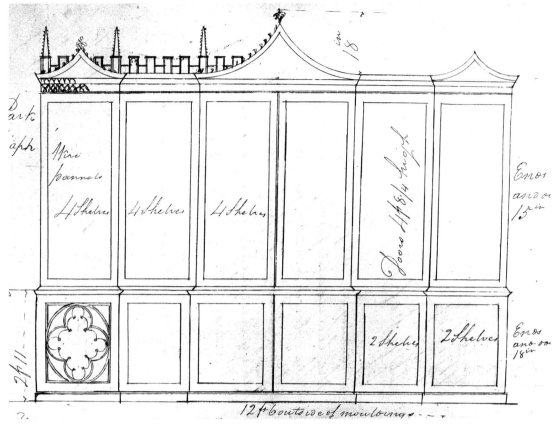

170   Library bookcase, 1795.

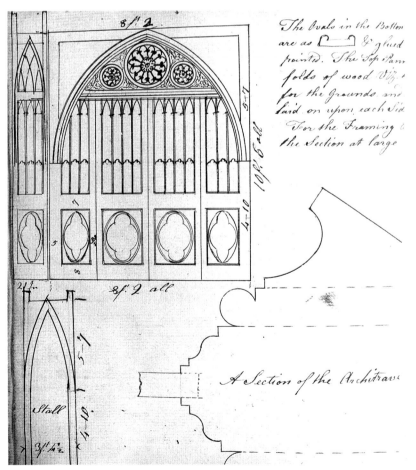

171   Gothic screen, 1798.

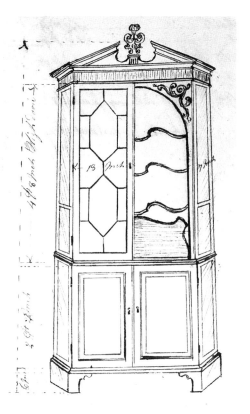

172   Buffet, 1787.

173   Corner cupboard, 1787.

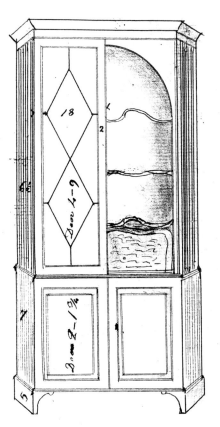

174   Buffet, 1798.

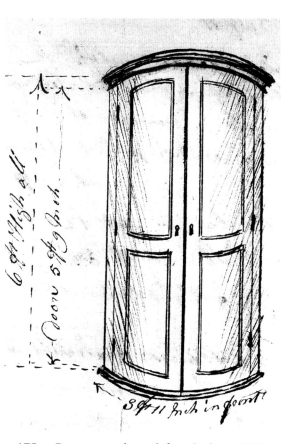

175   Corner cupboard for clothes, 1787.

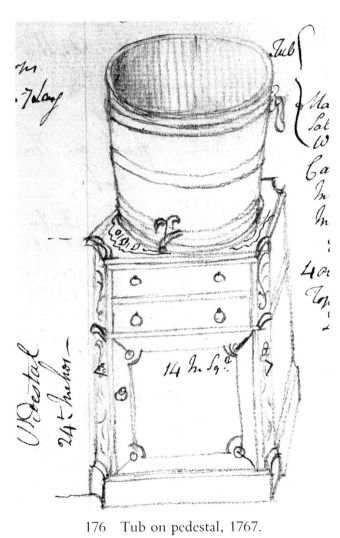

176   Tub on pedestal, 1767.

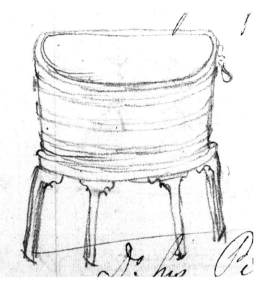

177   Cistern, 1767.

178   Cistern, 1787.

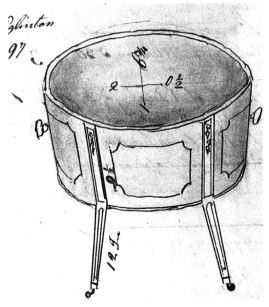

179   Cistern, 1799.

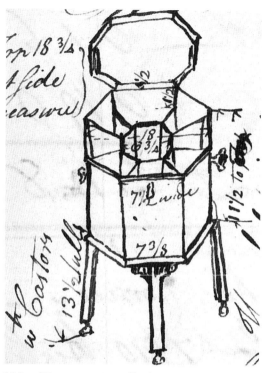

180 'Temporary cellar' or gardevine, 1769.

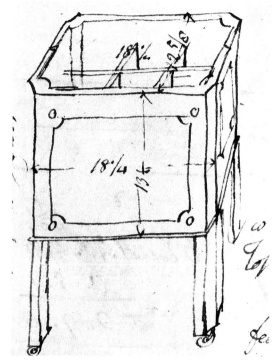

181 Gardevine, 1768.

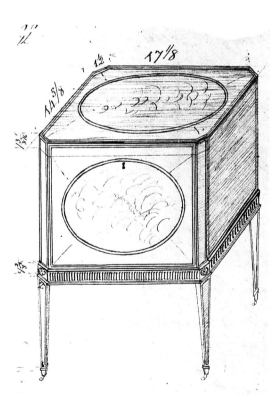

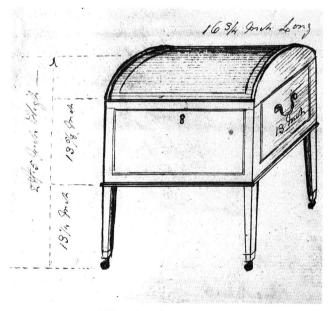

183 Gardevine, 1787.

182 Gardevine, 1788.

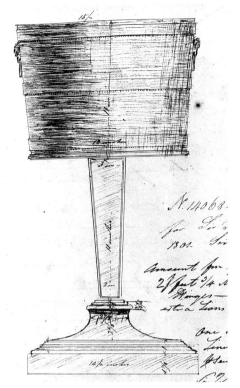
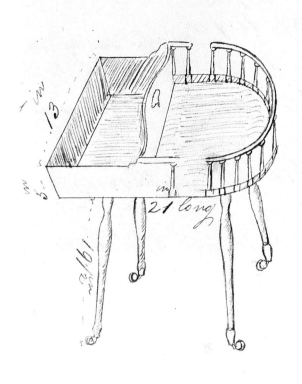

184   Tub on pedestal, 1790.   185   Knife box and plate basket, 1794.

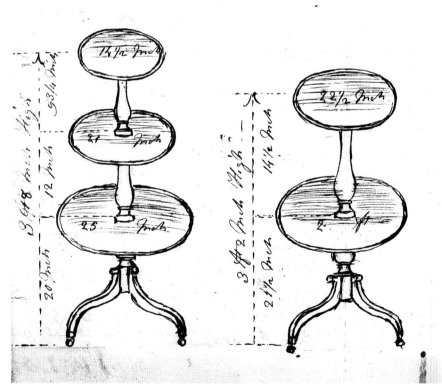

186   Dumb waiters, 1787.

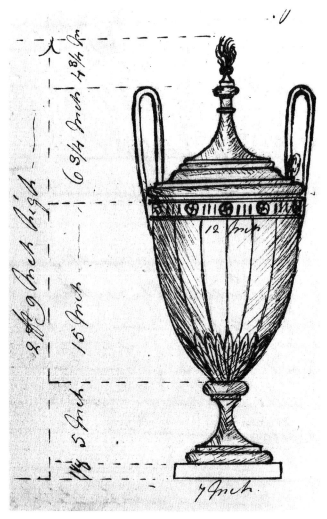

187   Vase with plated handles, 1788.

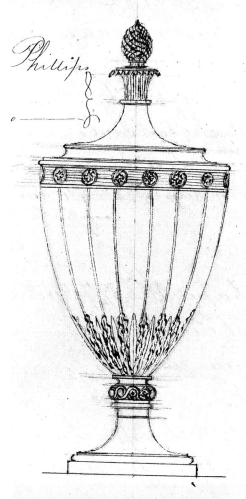

188   Vase knife case, 1796.

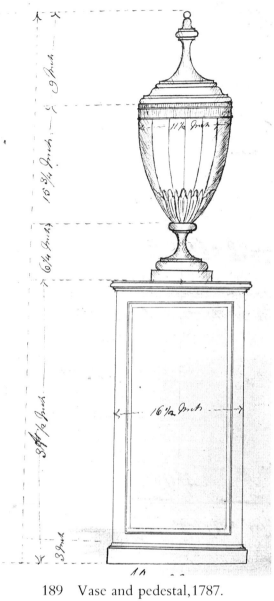

189   Vase and pedestal, 1787.

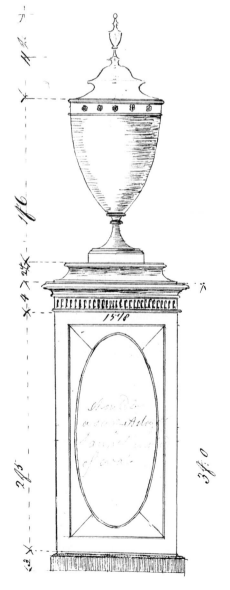

190   Vase knife case and pedestal, 1792.

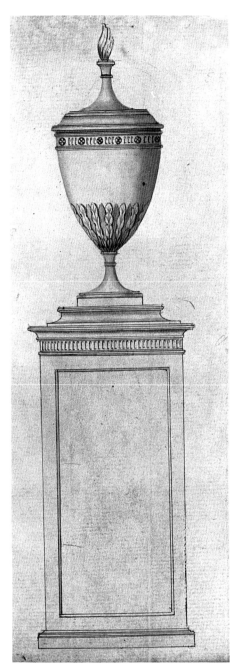

191   Vase and pedestal, 1788.

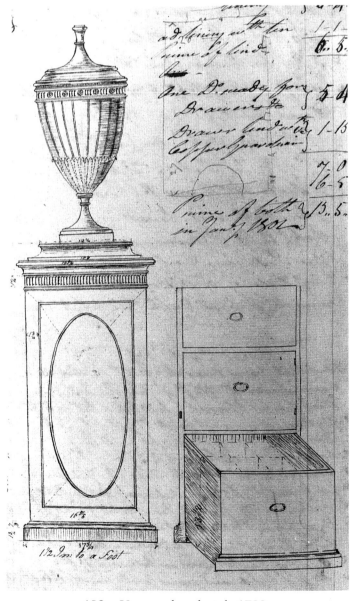

192   Vase and pedestal, 1788.

194 Swing glass, 1788.

193 Swing glass, 1759.

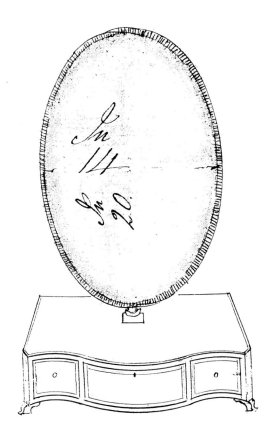

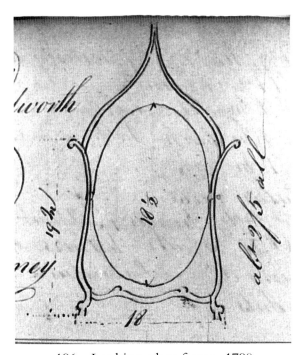

196 Looking-glass frame, 1790.

195 Oval looking-glass, 1797.

197 Pier glass frame, 1771.

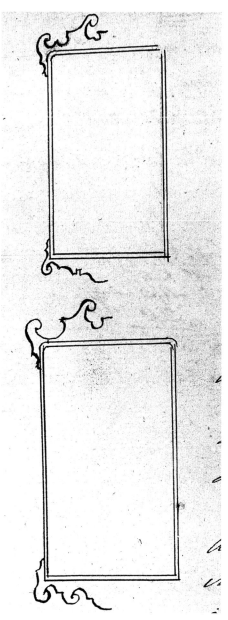

199 Two pier-glass frames, 1797.

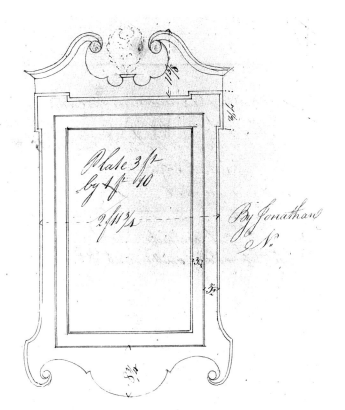

198 Pier glass frame, 1790.

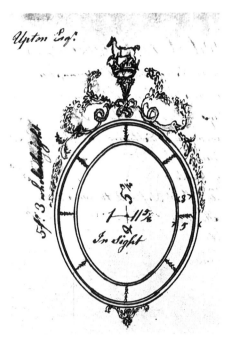

201 Pier glass frame, 1798.

200 Pier glass frame, 1788.

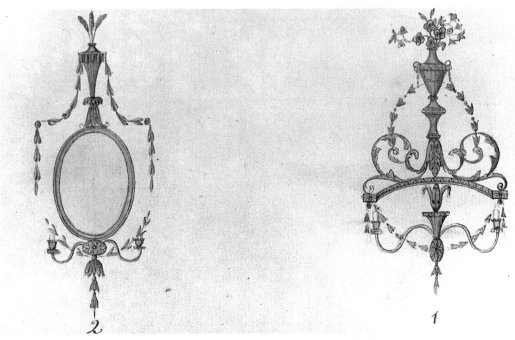

202 Girandoles, about 1790/1800.

203   Wall decoration, or surmount, about 1790/1800.

204   Gilt overmantel glass, 1792.

205   Pier glass, about 1790

206   Decorative surmount, about 1790/95.

207   Pier glass, about 1790/95.

208   Decorative surmount, about 1790/95.

209 Pier glass and table, about 1790

210 Girandoles, about 1790/95.

211   Pier glass, about 1790/95.

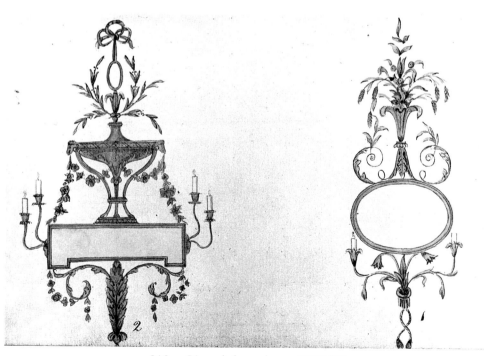

212   Girandoles, about 1790/95.

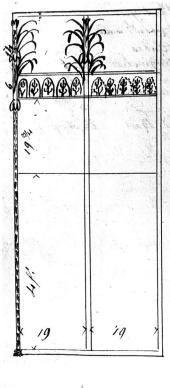

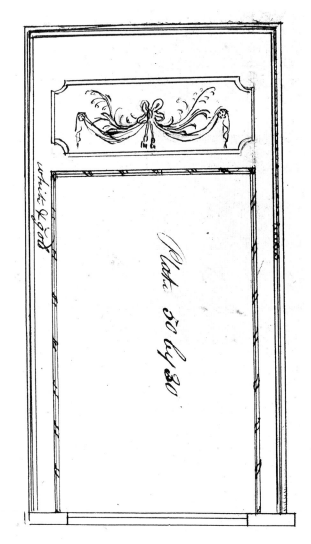

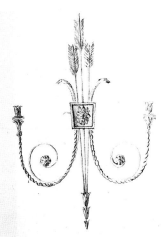

213   Pier glass frame, 1799.
214   Pier glass, 1794.

215   Girandole, about 1790.

216   Chimney glass, about 1790/95.

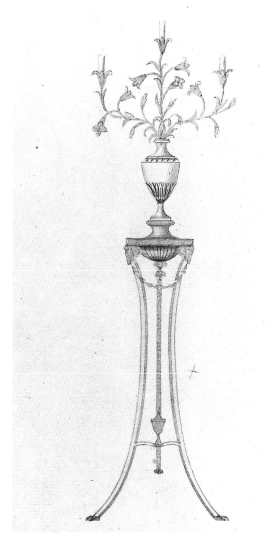

217   Tripod candlestand, about 1790/95.

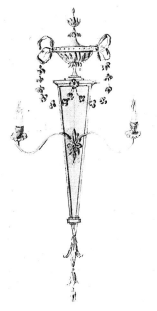

218   Girandoles, about 1790.   219   Girandole, about 1790.

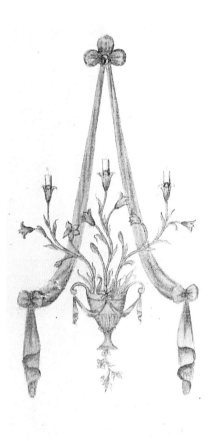

220   Girandole, about 1790.

221   Girandole, about 1790/95.

222   Decorative festoon and firescreens, about 1790.

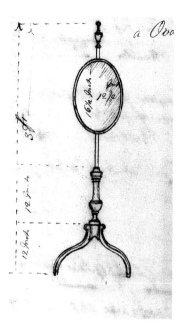

223   Firescreen, 1787.

224   Firescreen, 1796.

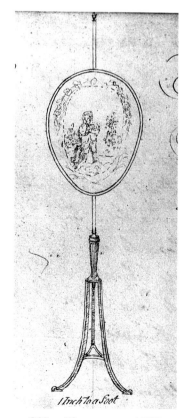

225   Firescreen, 1788.

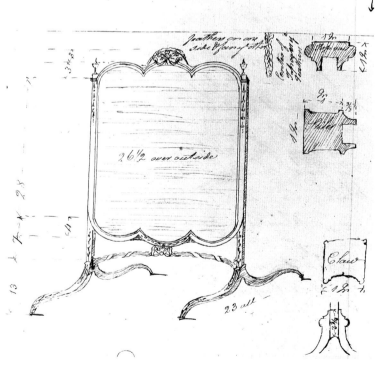

226   Firescreen, 1788.

227 Window cornice, 1787.

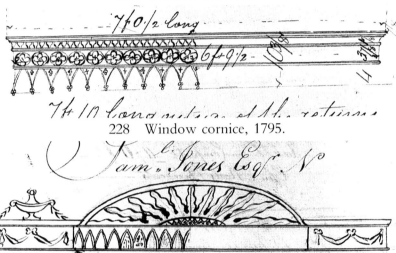

228 Window cornice, 1795.

229 Window cornice, 1789.

230 Window cornice and curtain, about 1790.

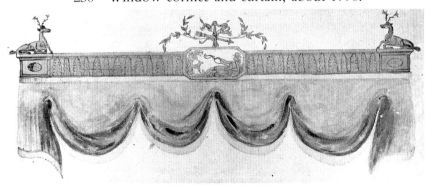

231 Window cornice and curtain, about 1790.

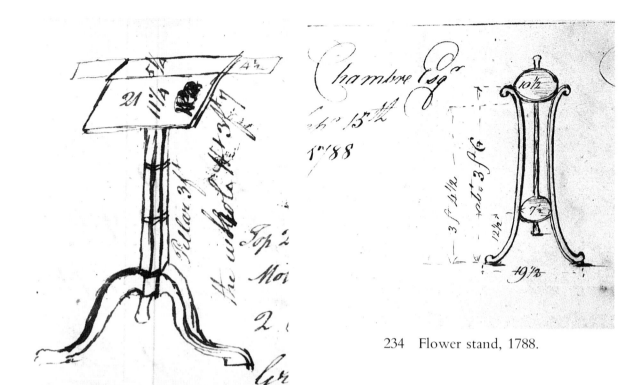

234 Flower stand, 1788.

232 Music or reading stand, about 1766/67.

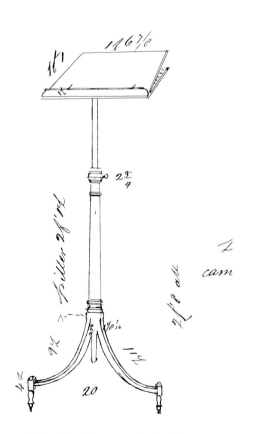

233 Reading stand, 1792.

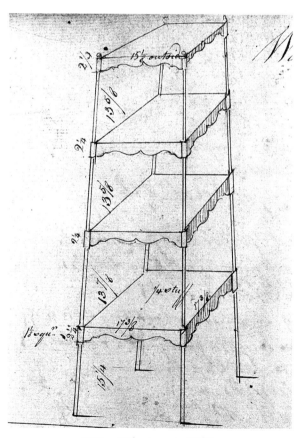

235 What-not, 1790.

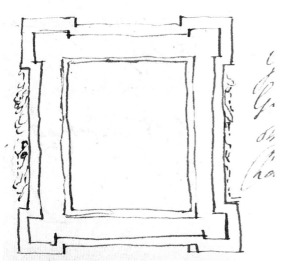

236　Picture-frame, 1767.

237　Gilt bracket, 1797.

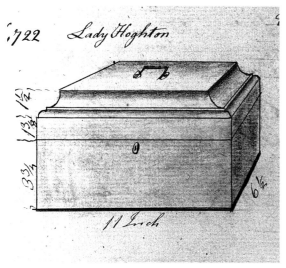

238　Tea-chest, 1798.

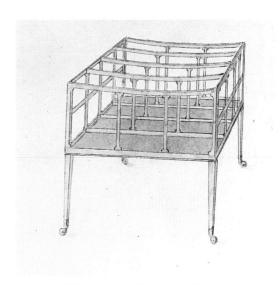

239　Canterbury, 1799/1802.

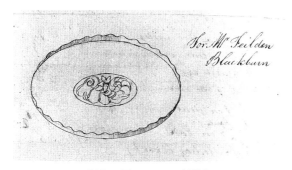

240　Tea tray, 1790.

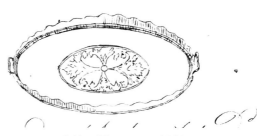

241　Tea tray, 1791.

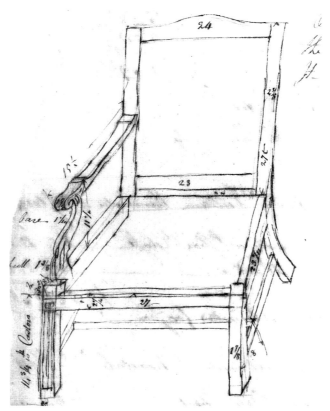

242   'French' armchair, 1761.

243   Splat–back settee, 1761.

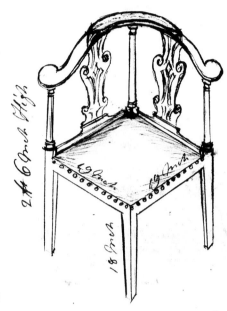

244　Smoking chair, 1787.

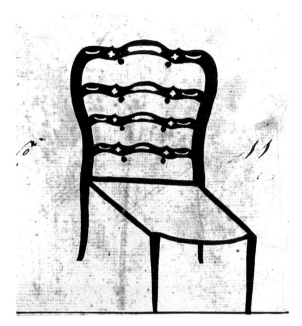

245　'Old splat back' chair, ?1770s.

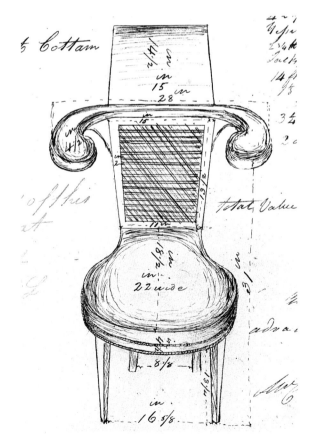

246　Reading chair, 1794.

247　Pierced splat ('ladderback') chair, 1769.

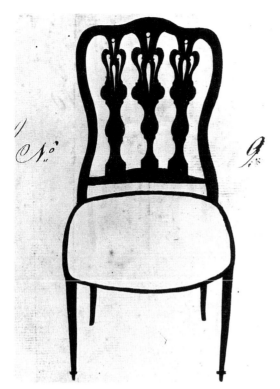

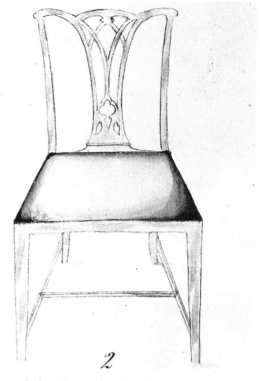

248 'Three upright baluster splats' chair, ? about 1775.

249 Carved splat chair, 1789.

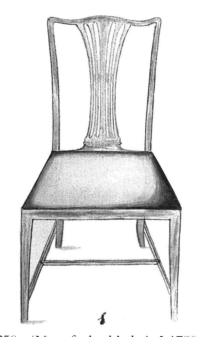

250 'New fanback' chair,? 1780s.

251 Fan-back chair.

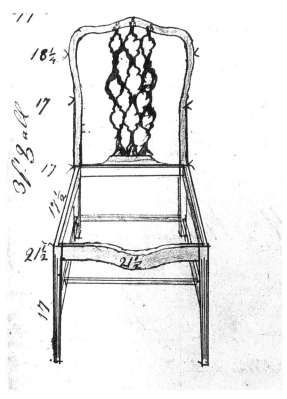

252 Chair with pierced splat, 1799.

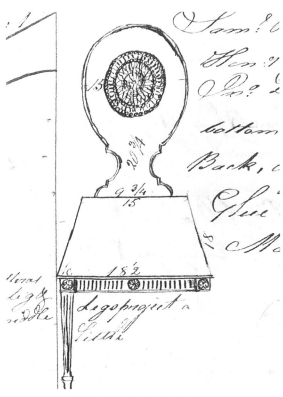

253 Hall chair, 1786.

254 Hall chair, 1788.

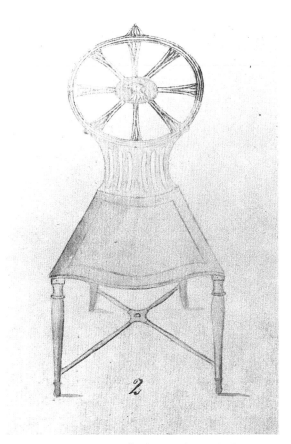

255 Hall chair, about 1790.

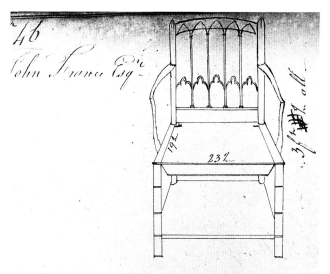

256 Gothic armchair, 1799.

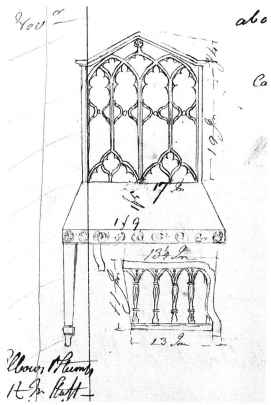

257 Gothic arch chair, 1784.

258 Chair simulating bamboo, 1794.

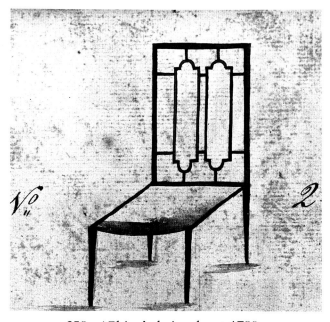

259 'China' chair, about 1790.

260 'Camel back' chair, about 1785/90.

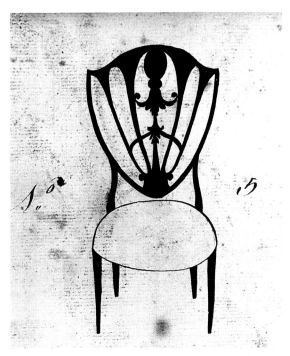

261 Shield-back chair, about 1785/90.

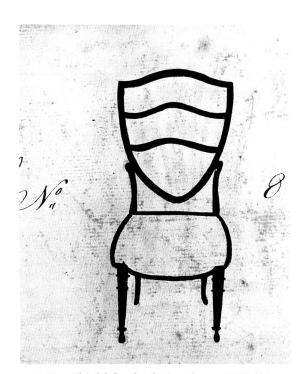

262 Shield-back chair, about 1785/90.

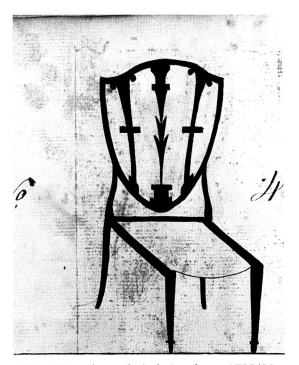

263 'Dog-leg splat' chair, about 1785/90.

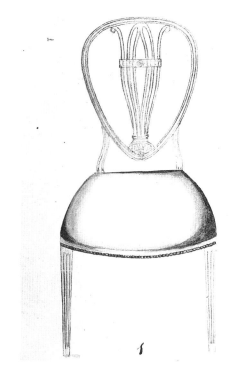

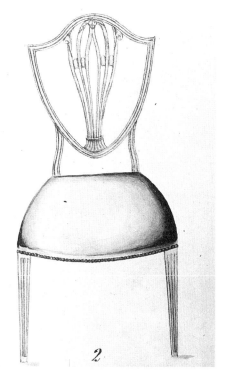

264 'Old balloon back' chair, 1785.

265 'New balloon back' chair, 1786.

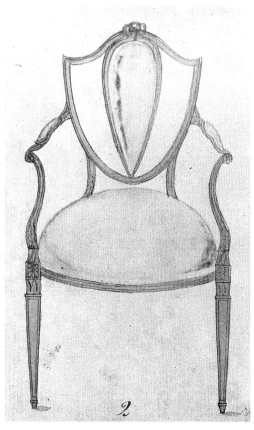

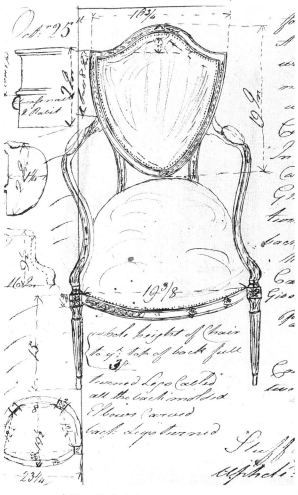

266 Shield-back chair, about 1785/90.

267 Cabriole armchair, 1786.

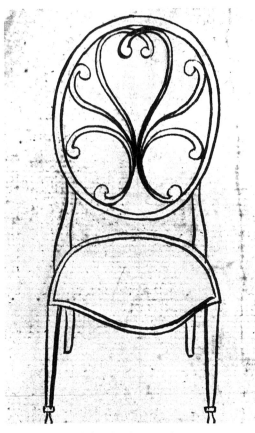

268 Oval-back chair, about 1785/90.

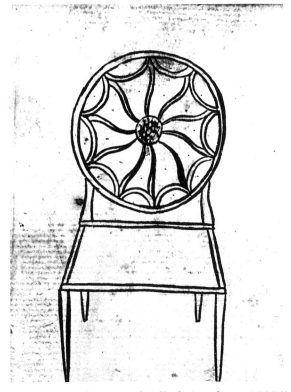

269 'New Catherine wheel' chair, about 1785/90.

270 Armchair, about 1785/90.

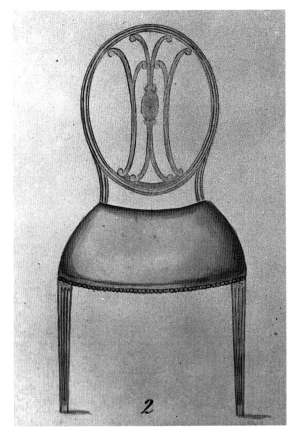

271 Oval-back chair, about 1785/90.

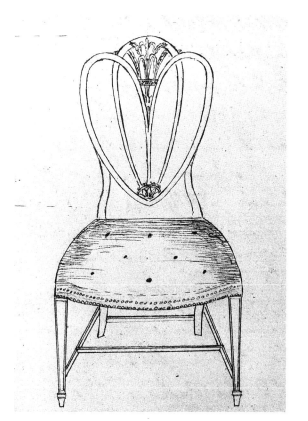

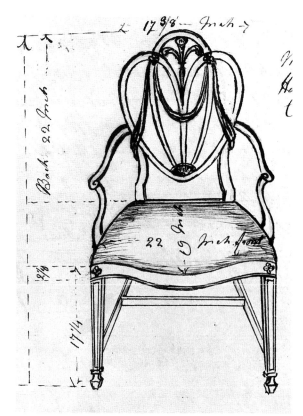

272   Dining-chair carved with wheatears, 1788.   273   Drapery and feather back armchair, 1788.

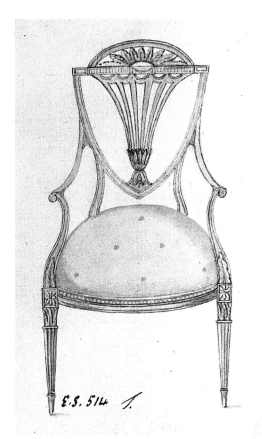

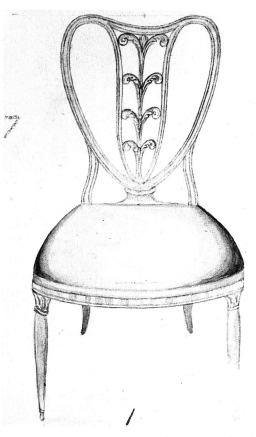

274   Armchair, 1789.

275   Wyatt's pattern chair, 1782/1791.

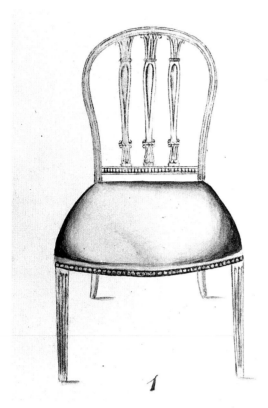

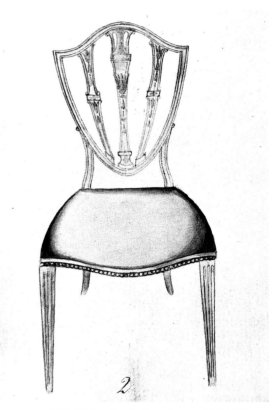

276　Three upright splats chair, 1791.

277　Shield-back chair, about 1785/90.

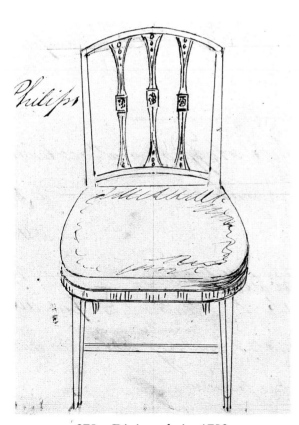

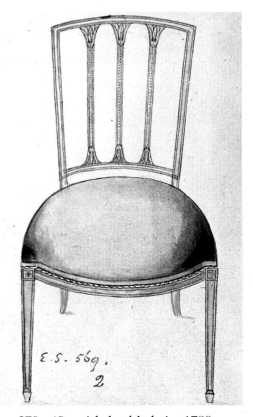

278　Dining-chair, 1793.

279　'Spanish-back' chair, 1789.

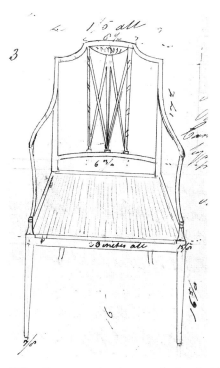

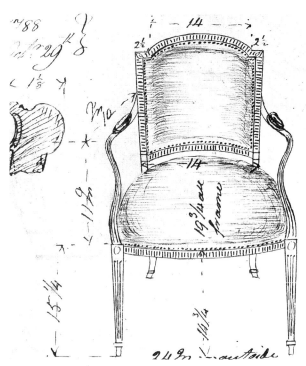

280 Lozenge-back armchair, 1792.

281 Cabriole armchair, 1788.

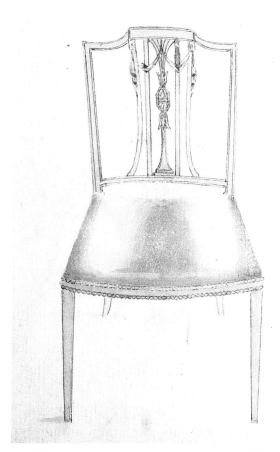

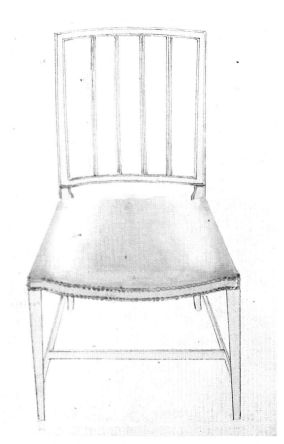

282 Dining/parlour chair, about 1790.

283 Dining/parlour chair, about 1790.

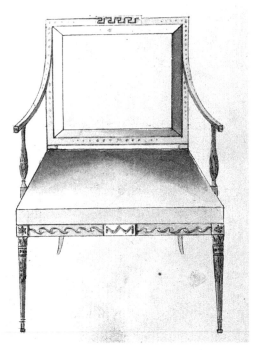

284   Armchair, about 1790/95.

285   Armchair, about 1790/95.

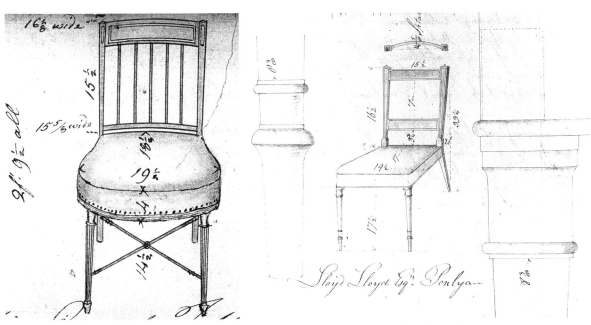

286   Tablet-back chair, 1797.

287   Dining/parlour chair, 1799.

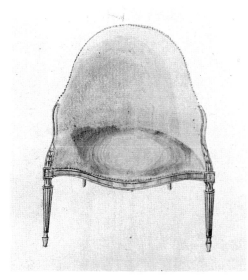

288   Armchair, about 1785/90.

289   'French' sofa, 1786.

290   Small sofa, 1787.

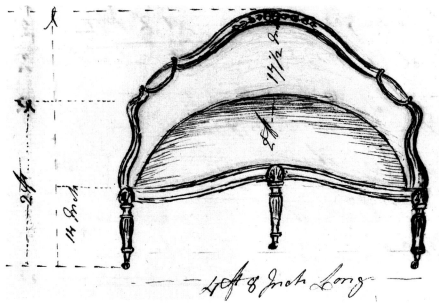

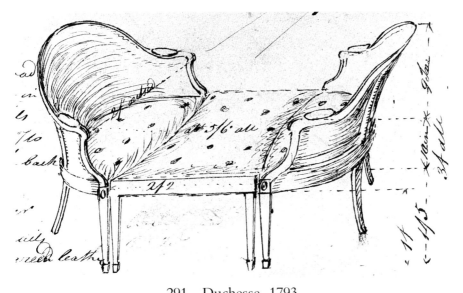

291   Duchesse, 1793

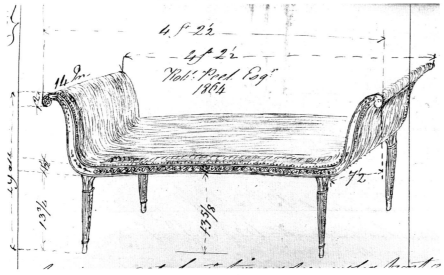

292   Stool, 1786.

293   'English' sofa, 1791.

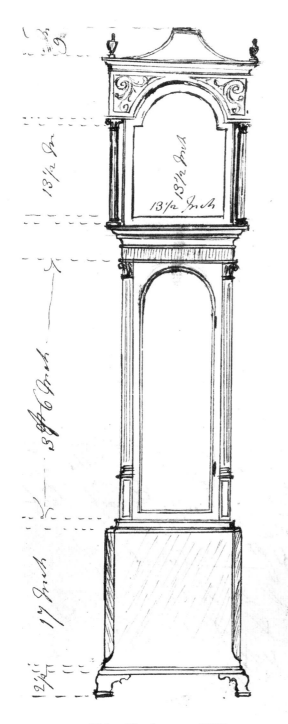

13½ in

13½ Inch

13½ Inch

3ft 6 Inch

1ft Inch

2½"

294 Clock case, 1787.

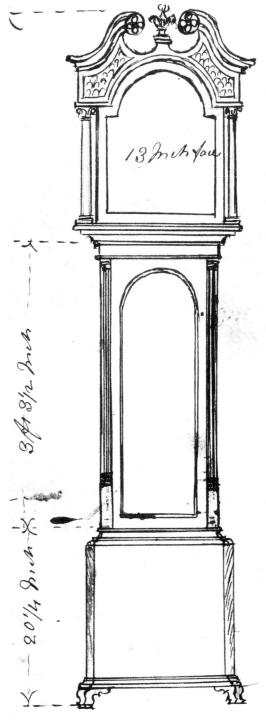

13 Inch face

3ft 8½ Inch

20¼ Inch

295 Clock case, 1787.

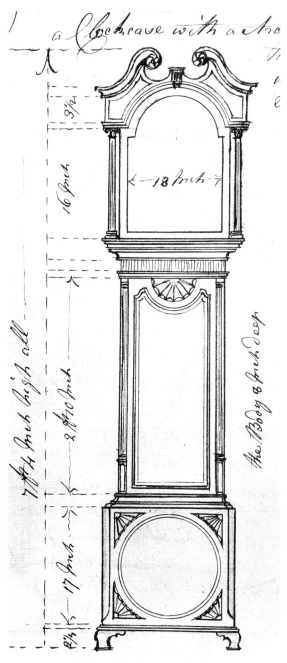

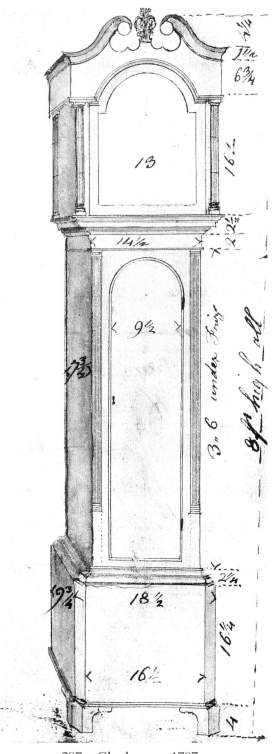

296   Clock case, 1788.

297   Clock case, 1797.

298   Watch–case, 1789.

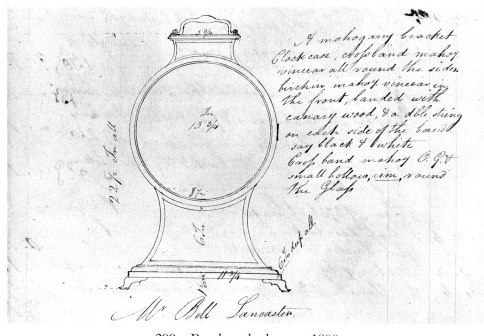

299   Bracket clock case, 1800.

1   Two pier/card tables, about 1785/90.

2   Two square tables, about 1785/90.

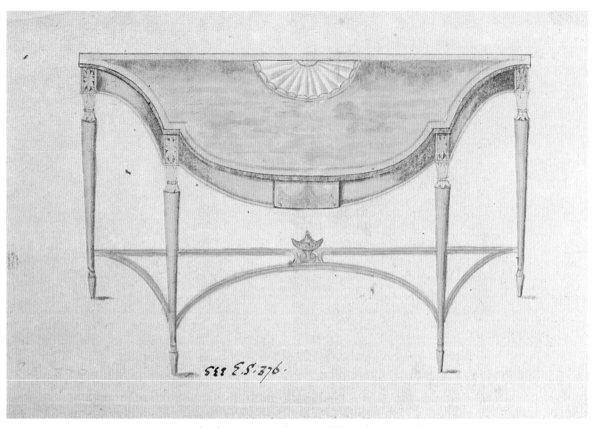

3   Inlaid satinwood pier table, about 1788.

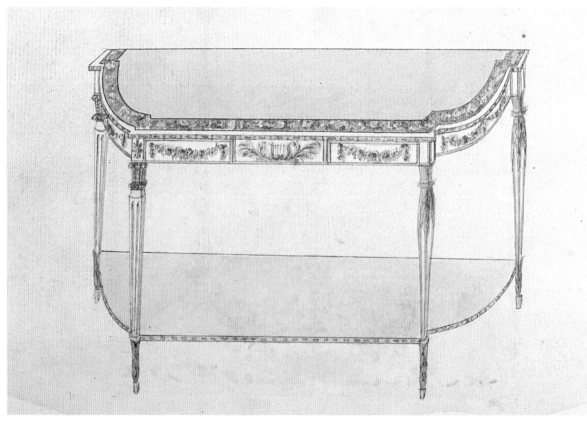

4   Pier table, about 1795.

5   Satinwood writing-table 1794.

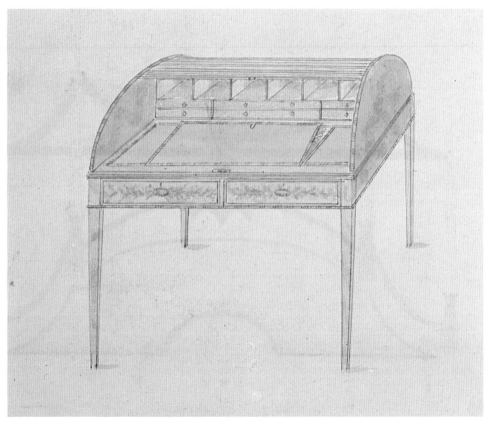

6   Satinwood writing-table, about 1790/95.

7   Satinwood secretaire with painted decoration, about 1798.

8   Cabinet, mahogany and purplewood, about 1789.

9   Cabinet, canarywood, about 1795.

10   Satinwood secretaire, about 1789.

11   Satinwood chest of drawers, about 1789.

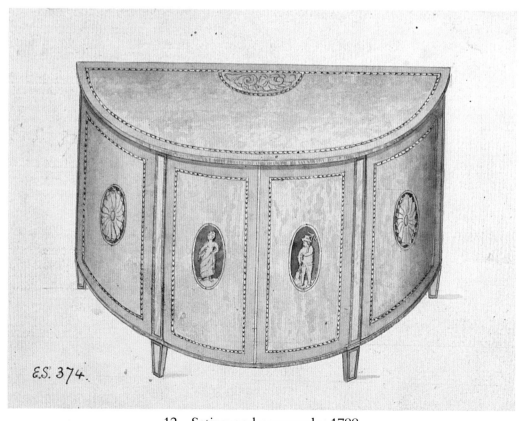

E.S. 374.

12   Satinwood commode, 1788.

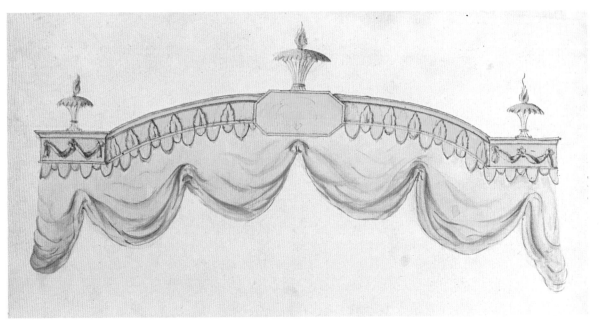

13   Window-cornice, about 1785/90.

14   Satinwood secretaire and globe, about 1790/95.

15   Three window-cornices, about 1785/90.

16   Three window-cornices, about 1785/90.

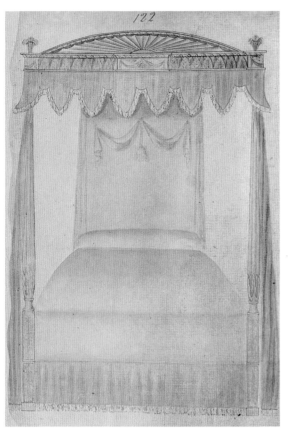

17　Four-poster bed, about 1790.

18　Couch bed, about 1788.

19   Alcove bed, about 1793.

20   Window-curtains, pier-glass and table, about 1792.

21 Pier-glass frame, about 1790/95.

116

22 Pier-glass frame, about 1790/95.

23   Detail of pier-glass.

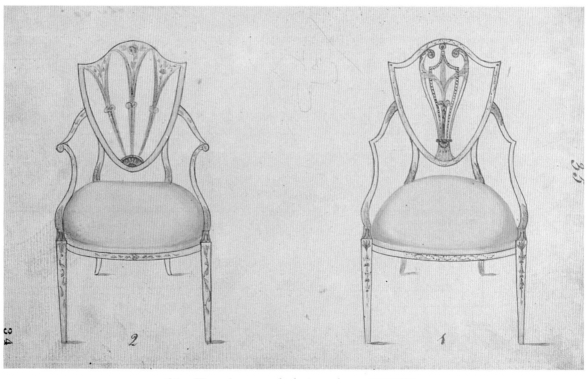

24   Two japanned chairs, about 1785/90.

25   'English' sofa, about 1790.

26   'French' sofa, about 1785/90.

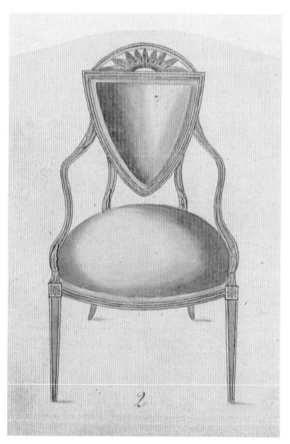
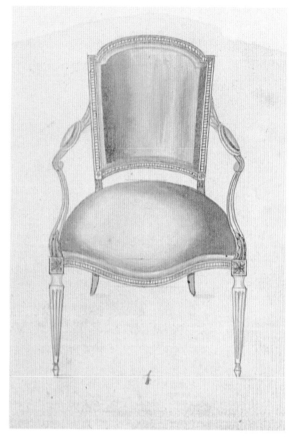

27 Two chairs (A) about 1789 (B) about 1788.

28 Two chairs (A) about 1790 (B) about 1797.

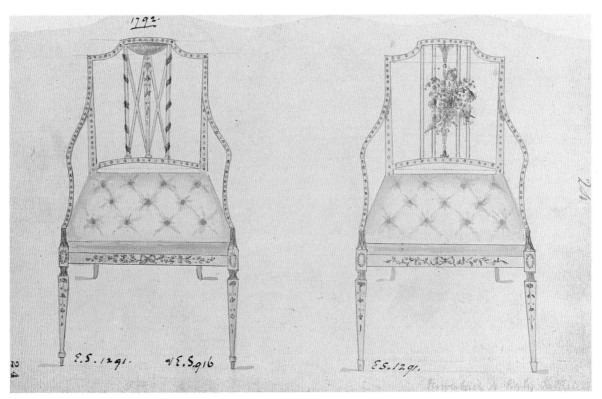

29   Two chairs (A) 1790s (B) about 1796.

30   Two chairs (A) about 1795/1800 (B) about 1795.

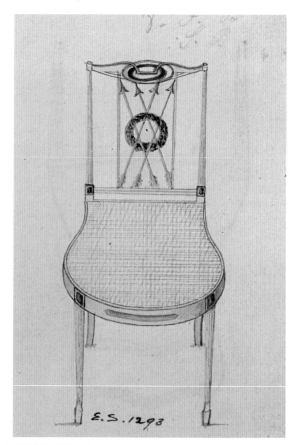

31   Two chairs (A) about 1785/90 (B) about 1795.

32   Two chairs (A) about 1785/90 (B) about 1790/95.

Where no other wood is indicated mahogany is to be understood.

1 Card table [1762] with folding frame, gothic legs &c., available with or without carved edge; made by W.T. [?William Townley], 8 days ('Huit Jour') 7½ hours (89/77).

2 Universal table, i.e. card, backgammon and chequer table with three tops, dated 22.12.1761; gothic legs, brackets, fret on rail; for Mr Thomas Wilson of Kendal (89/64).

3 Universal table [about September 1760], for Mr Chippendale, attorney at Manchester (89/26).

4 Universal table [May 1787], the top 2'8" × 2'7" (94/4).

5 Card table, dated 26.11.1787: the rails panelled with a purple band and the top banded; the legs tapered and fluted; a vase [unclear whether carved or inlaid] on the tablet; H 2'4" × 3'2" × 17" (94/106).

6 Card table (one of a pair) dated [15].2.1787, for Edward Standish: satinwood, for the drawing-room at Standish Hall, Lancs.; top and edges crossbanded with tulipwood and white angles, a black and white string round inside of inlaid margin, tablet inlaid with a vase and crossbanded with tulipwood, rails longbanded with purplewood, projecting legs with inlaid blue and yellow ovals at the top and inlaid green husks, also purplewood angles, a satinwood longband round the bottom of the rail; 3'3¾" × 18½"; made by Henry Walwin and inlaid by John Dowbiggin, no. 2165 (93/500).

7 Card table [August 1794], for the London shop: mahogany, the top crossbanded with kingwood, a white band and two black strings inside the crossband, the front edge crossbanded with tulipwood, the rails strung in five panels, the top ends of legs strung in panels with hollow corners, the legs strung on ten sides; H 29⅛" × 3' L. Made by John Savage (96/1112).

8 Card table, dated 23.5.1797: satinwood, the top with a margin of zebrawood and black and white string, 1¼" broad, the rails and legs panelled with a small black thread, the tops of the legs with a purplewood lozenge, and a white string on each angle of the top. H 2'4½" × 3' × 1'5½". Made by I. Robinson (97/1348).

9 Card table, dated 19.4.1784, for Edmund Craddock Hartopp of Merevale Hall, Warwickshire; satinwood, the upper part veneered on oak and inlaid with various colours, also crossbanded with tulipwood; legs cabled, capitals carved. H 2'6½" × 3'9" × 1'9". Made by 'young' Robert Edmundson (93/40). see Fig. 61 for matching pembroke table.

10 Pier table, dated 25.4.1793, for — Asheton, Esq., no. 19,487; satinwood, japanned; top crossbanded and strung with two angles; rails longbanded with ebony and strung; legs projecting and a band with two strings broken over; 4' × 21"; made by S. Cooper (96/965).

11 Pier table, dated 3.12.1788, for John Christian Esq. of Workington Hall, Cumberland, no. 8014; mahogany, paterae carved out of the solid, carved capitals with leaves under, legs carved and panelled on ten sides, top veneered and two white angles and a white string in the middle of the edge, rails crossbanded and a longband on the bottom edge; top veneered on oak, oak back rail, deal cross rail; H 3' + 1½" + 3½" + 3⅝" × 4'6"; made by T.Atkinson, legs carved and sunk by Baylie, varnished by Joynson (94/448).

12 Pier table, [October 1793], for Mr Murrey, no. 20,024; satinwood, inlaid shaded shell (not shown, but specified in Waste Book), new and ordinary stringing; H 3' × 4'4"; made by P.Briscoe, painted by Wilkes (96/1022).

13 Pier table, dated 21.8.1788, no. 8008;

for John Christian, Esq.; mahogany, carved tablet, legs, and paterae; legs sunk, husks on three sides, broad purplewood band and shaded stringing round top, inlaid shell on top; rails in panels, purplewood crossbands, legs projecting; H 3' × 4'9" × 20"; made by Henry Walling (94/372).

14 Pier table, dated 22.8.1788, for John Christian Esq., of Workington Hall, Cumberland; satinwood, the top crossbanded with purplewood and a shaded string round, inlaid shell and a shaded string round, edge of top crossbanded with kingwood, white angles, tablet broken and longbanded round with purplewood, purplewood longband on bottom edge of rail; rails veneered longways on deal; stretching rail veneered on oak; japanned with drapery in the tablet, paterae on the legs, flutes on the rail, husks and lines on the legs, all green, also purple bands &c.; H 3' × 5'4¾" × 1'9"; scale about 1" to 1'; made by C. Procter (94/376).

15 Pier table ('new'), dated 22.11.1790, no. 14,440; mahogany, drawer fronts longbanded with ebony and strung and white angles; four plain round legs projecting and mouldings broken over; top longbanded with ebony and white angles bent round columns; mouldings round shelf broken over legs at back and the edge of the rim of the shelf longbanded with ebony and with two angles; H 2'11¼" × 4'6½" × 18"; made by James Burton (95/675).

16 Pier table, dated 30.9.1789, for John Trafford, Esq., of Trafford Park, Lancs.; mahogany; H 2'10¼" × 4'10½" × 1'8"; waterleaves are drawn faintly in pencil under the frieze at 2; made by R. Gibson (95/531).

17 Pier table, dated 11.9.1795 for Mr. Abraham Crompton of Chorley Hall, Lancs.; deal, the fronts of mahogany, the drawers of cedar; japanned white ground, oval landscape in the middle, a painted border round the top, swags of yellow drapery painted on the front; H 33" × 4'10" x 25½"; made by F. Dowbiggin, painted by James Hutton (97/1195).

18 Pier table (but called commode in the Waste Book), dated 13.6.1795; one of three for Wilbraham Bootle, Esq., of Lathom Hall, Lancs., no. 32,786; mahogany; the top drawer with a slide, a plain cupboard at each end; the frieze at the ends opening with the doors; the door fronts veneered with 'birchings' but without bands or strings; H 3' × 4'7" × 26/28"; made by I. Robinson, the other two by Townson and Drape (97/1170).

19 'A large, neat & strong Writing Table, a Library Table', Nov.1767; mahogany, oak; note the lettered drawers (90/65).

20 Library table, dated 25.2.1768, 'for Hull': although Gillows had customers named Hull, in this case the port seems indicated, judging from a previous piece sent to Messrs Watson of Hull; the top veneer centrematched with 'birching' figure, featherbanded and crossbanded (90/80).

21 Library table, dated 18.7.1792, for Sir John Ramsden, of Byram Hall, Yorks.; mahogany, black leather top; a kingwood crossband 2⅞" all round top; eight columns inlaid with ebony flutes; 20 brass handles from London; sham front behind; H 2'6" × 3'6" × 6'; made by Robert Clarkson and John Hesseldon (96/872).

22 Bureau and bookshelf, dated 19.6.1795, for Gore Townshend, Esq., of Honington Hall, Warwickshire, no. 32,712; the top to elevate both ways like a bureau top; square handles; made by J. Hodgson (97/1174).

23 Writing table with elevating top [May–June 1787], no. 4223; H 2'11" × 24¾" × 24¾". Made by James Burton (94/45).

24 Bureau writing-table, dated 21.3.1789, no. 9833, for the Earl of Shrewsbury; mahogany, with rising top; H 2'10" × 4' × 24¾"; leather top, lettered covers; made by T. Blackburn (95/480).

25 Circular library table, dated 26.9.1789, for J.F. Cawthorne, Esq., (written 'Cawthore' on sketch); mahogany; made by W. Getskell, lettered by T. Romney (95/528).

26 Circular library table, dated 24.2.1792, no. 17,440; mahogany, made by W. Lupton (96/834).

27 Circular writing-table, dated 16.9. 1795, sent to the London shop for George Smith, Esq., no. 33,297; mahogany, made by John Hodgson (97/1195).

28 Deception table [June–July] 1787; H 2'5½" × 2' × 14¼" + flap 8⅜" (94/44–5)

29 Dressing-table, dated 1.9.1770, for Mrs. Plante of Norfolk Street, London via the London shop; mahogany; made by James Robinson, William Lupton, and Bryan Overend; note the 'open cross rail' (90/149).

30 Small dressing-table, dated June 1792, for the Bishop of St. Asaph, no. 17,794; mahogany, made by Robert Fell (96/858).

31 Dressing-table, dated 24.8.1789, for Sir William Milner of Nun Appleton Hall, Yorks.; mahogany; H 2'8½" × 2'6¼" × 18½"; made by C. Procter (95/518).

32 Lady's circular dressing-table, May 1787, no. 4068; diameter 3'2¾" × H 2'8½" (94/2).

33 Dressing-table, dated 6.8.1794, for W.W. Carus, Esq., no. 31,394; made by B. Townson (96/1109).

34 Dressing-table [September 1791]; mahogany; made by William Atkinson and James Burton (95/774).

35 Writing-table, dated 20.1.1790, for the London shop, no. 12,267; also called 'a library table to stand in the middle of a room'; new sort of writing drawer with top front to fall, rising flap on slide, six hinged covers, private drawers &c., black ebony bands, a broad purplewood band round top, sham doors at the back and sham fronts; H 3' × 4'1¼" × 2'3½"; made by John Savage (95/558).

36 Dressing-table, dated 25.5.1790, for Mr. Unsworth [presumably of Maghull Hall, Lancs.,], no. 12,819; japanned, H 2'6" × 4' × 20"; made by William Atkinson and japanned by Thomas Knight (95/599).

37 Dressing-table, undated but about 1790; concave ('hollow') front, oval handles, canted corners (735/1, f.89).

38 Dressing-table (but called a pier table in the Waste Book), dated 18.7.1795, for George Briscoe of Stourbridge, no. 32,926; mahogany, made by F. Dowbiggin (97/1181).

39 Kidney writing-table, dated 24.11. 1787, for Lord Stourton; mahogany, banded with kingwood, and strung with white; the top covered with cloth; H 2'5" × 3'2" × 15½"; made by William Brisco (94/156).

40 Kidney writing-table, dated September 1792, for John Dumbell, Esq., no. 17,938; mahogany; H 28" × 4'6" × 3'6"; made by T. Romney (96/896).

41 Writing-table, dated 12.1.1794, for J. Shuckburgh, Esq.; satinwood, new sort of bureau writing-drawer, a rising flap on slide with ink and sand bottles, plain solid hinged covers, top veneered on oak, a broad purplewood band round the top, the fronts banded and strung with purplewood, black angles in the legs, the ends veneered on oak, a satinwood moulding round the top; no. 30,353, made by Robert Fell (96/1054). See also Colour Plate 5.

42 Harlequin writing-table, [May 1791], no. 16,142; satinwood, with a screen behind 'same as a shever de frise table'; top covered in green leather, crossbanded with tulipwood, the edge crossbanded with kingwood; black angles in the legs; the projecting legs banded with tulipwood; made by T. Romney (95/728).

43 A 'Watson's' writing-table, dated 19.1. 1799, for the Earl of Eglinton; satinwood, also mahogany and cedar; the top panelled with purplewood and double strung, the edge banded with purplewood and with black and white angles, the drawer fronts banded with purplewood and a double black and white string; a slide at each end for candles; ivory knobs; ink and sand bottles in top right-hand drawer; made by Isaac Robinson (98/1497).

44 Writing-table with upper section containing a cupboard and drawers; undated, about 1790/95; note the stretching-rail (735/1, f.8).

45 Writing-table and bookshelf, undated, about 1790/95; note the stretching-rail and handle for the detachable top section (735/1, f.86).

46 Writing-table, dated 27.7.1795, sent to the London shop; made in two parts, the bottom forming a complete table; the top of the bottom part veneered and a broad canarywood and mahogany band all round the outside, the edge banded with tulipwood and white strings all round; the rails veneered, longbanded with canarywood and strung in six panels, the top ends of the legs strung in eight square panels. The convex forms of the junction of front and ends were called 'sash corners' by Gillows. Made by Peter Briscoe (97/1186).

47 Cylinder writing-desk, dated 16.7.1796, sent to the London shop for 'a friend of Mr. Pilling's', no. 34,779; satinwood, the top and drawers longbanded with purplewood and strung, the rolling slide banded twice with purplewood and double strung; the edge of the top and edge of the cylinder ends banded with tulipwood and strung; tulipwood at letters A and B continued on the ends and square pilasters; each end strung in three panels, the top ends of the pilasters in six square panels and six ditto below A, rounded at top ends, purplewood tablet for the desk; H 3'5" × 3' × 22¾", made by Peter Brisco (97/1252).

48 Writing-table with reeded top, dated 15.9.1787, for Messrs. E. & G. Suart; the front and small drawers inside banded with purplewood and strung with white, the legs ditto; H 3'10" × 4'2" × 2'8"; no. 5884, made by John Savage, the lettering and varnishing by John Dowbiggin (94/102). For a similar table dated 12.10.1789 (3' long) see 95/537.

49 Cylinder writing-desk, dated 1.9.1794; mahogany, the tablet for the mortice lock veneered with purplewood and crossbanded; the doors with wire and green silk curtains; H 2'7½" + 11½" + 12" + 6" × 3'

× 23" (lower)/12½" (middle)/9" (upper); made by C. Lupton (96/1115).

50 'Carlton House' writing-table, dated 12.6.1798, for the Earl of Derby, no. 37,034; the drawer fronts crossbanded with kingwood and strung; made by S.Cooper. A note refers to f.1245 for a similar table previously made by W. Beckett, which was called a 'writing table', with 'Carleton House' added subsequently in different ink above the sketch (97/1453).

51 Oval dining table, dated 22.10.1796, for Thomas Hind Jnr. of Liverpool, no. 35,232; H 29" × 4' × 20⅝" + two flaps 22"; mahogany, made by G. Atkinson (97/1284).

52 Corner table, [about September 1768 or early 1769] (90/111).

53 Breakfast table, dated 11.12.1794, ordered by and sent to the London shop for Henry Tomkinson, Esq., of Dorfold Hall, Cheshire, but probably for his London house; no. 32,136; mahogany, the top veneered on mahogany, with a joint; the astragal moulding on the edge and bottom of the top rails veneered on oak; fluted legs; H 29" × 4'6" × 3'3"; made by George Atkinson (96/1138).

54 Set of dining tables, dated 27.9.1788, for the London shop; mahogany; made by William Gaskell (94/412).

55 Set of dining tables, dated 6.8.1788, for Lady Blount of Bellamour, Staffs., no. 37,284; mahogany; made by G.Atkinson (98/1465).

56 Set of dining tables, dated 7.8.1791, for Sir Walter Blount, of Mawley Hall, Salop, no. 16,463; mahogany, made by T.Blackburn (95/760).

57 Small table with term legs, dated April 1766; mahogany; made by William Lupton (90/10).

58 'Fly table', dated April 1770, for Colonel Townley [probably Richard Townley of Belfield Hall, Lancs.], with cross-rail (90/137).

59 Pembroke table, dated March 1772, fitted with ink and sand bottles; note the cross-rail, as in Fig. 58 (90/200).

60 Oval pembroke table, dated 4.10. 1788, for John Christian, no. 7093; intended for a dressing-room, but unclear whether for Workington Hall or Belle Isle; top 3'5" × 3'; rails 3⅞" deep; green bands at the bottom with purplewood longband and string round them, a purplewood oval at the top of the legs and purplewood angles in the legs, the top crossbanded round ¾" broad and with a shaded string round, also a shaded string round the centre inlaid oval shell; made by T. Atkinson (94/414).

61 Pembroke table, dated 19.4.1784, for Edmund Craddock Hartopp of Merevale Hall, Warwickshire, to match his card table (see Fig. 9); top about 3'6" × 2'6"; satinwood veneered on mahogany, inlaid with coloured woods, and with tulipwood bands (93/41).

62 Pembroke table, dated 25.7.1794, for Mrs. Horton, no. 31,277; mahogany, top longbanded and strung, drawer front and end longbanded and strung, black and white string broken over bottom edge of rails and over the legs, legs strung in panels on eight sides, top ends of legs strung in panels with 'hollow corners' (i.e. a concave depression at the angle); made by R. Gibson (96/1104).

63 Pembroke table, dated 16.4.1793, no. 19,299; mahogany, with cabled legs, carved capitals, and sunk paterae; made by William Beckett (96/963, but this taken from the better-drawn version in 735/1, f.127).

64 Pembroke games table, dated 25.8. 1793, for the London shop; made by T. Escolme (96/1033).

65 Pembroke table and library ladder, dated 10.2.1798, for John Christian Curwen, Esq. Drawing, making moulds, and making by T. Romney (97/1420).

66 Snap table on pillar and claw, dated 28.12.1787; mahogany; H 2'4" × 2'11¼" diameter (94/224).

67 Work table on pillar and claw, dated 1.3.1798, for Sir Thomas Hesketh of Rufford New Hall, Lancs., no. 36,929; made by Robert ('Bob') Townson (97/1425).

68 Circular snap table on pillar and claw, dated 27.1.1798, for Sir Thomas Hesketh (see note 67), no. 36,759; 3'6" diameter, the top of mahogany veneered with fine satinwood and a crossband of kingwood and stringing, with an astragal edge stained black and a black string on each angle of the pillar and top angle of the claws; made by John Kilner (97/1415).

69 Octagon snap table on pillar and claw, dated 27.1.1798, for Sir Thomas Hesketh (see note 67); description as note 68, but 3'4" diameter; also by Kilner (97/1415).

70 Tea 'Kitchen' (Kettle) stand, about May 1769, for Thomas Willis, Esq.; made by William Ball and Richard Gibson (90/115).

71 Tea table, dated 7.12.1767, for Messrs. Watson; baluster gallery, serpentine top, tapering legs with carved brackets in the angles (90/69).

72 Tea table, about May 1767, for Mr. Bateman; made by William Lupton, the claws carved by James Townson (90/55).

73 Tea table, dated 22.9.1786, for John Carstens of Hamburg, no. 1120; mahogany, the 'tray top' veneered on oak; H 2'6" × 2'8" × 2'; made by John Wainhouse, carved by John Dowbiggin (93/417).

74 Lady's work table, dated 24.7.1788, for Jeremiah Dixon, Esq.; whitewood painted, claws moulded; poplar, oak, and beech; H 2'4" × 18" diameter; made by Thomas Romney (94/350).

75 Three work tables sliding to form a 'nest' dated 9.2.1795; sent to the London shop, no. 32,326; mahogany; made by I. Robinson (97/1144).

76 Octagon work table [September–October] 1794, for the Wareroom (showroom); satinwood, blue silk bag; made by

R. Lister, varnished and polished by T. Romney (96/1120).

77 Work table on frame, dated 15.6.1795, for John Barton of Manchester, no. 32,675; mahogany, with crossband, white string, white angles; H 30⅞" × 19⅛" × 15⅛"; made by T. Romney (97/1171).

78 Work-bag table, [October 1793], for Satterthwaite, no. 20,082; satinwood; made by Robert Fell (96/1027).

79 Frame for a marble top: one of a pair, dated 2.11.1795, for William Egerton of Tatton Park, Cheshire; mahogany, gilded; made by Thomas Romney and Duke Ball, gilded by Thomas Dobson (97/1206).

80 Sideboard table, July 1771, for Miss Gibson; the rails veneered with 'birching' figure mahogany (90/182).

81 Sideboard table, dated 10.4.1770, for Col. Townley (see note 58); the top of fine wood; carved tablet (90/136).

82 Plate case, November 1767, for Mr. Moss of Preston; 4'6" long; note the 'hollow corners' and paterae, also the plinth (90/66).

83 Sideboard, dated 29.10.1787, for Mr. Robert Worswick; mahogany, Danzig oak, with shaded stringing and purplewood veneer; H 2'10" × 4'10½" × 20¼"; made by William Beckett, the drawer front fluted by Thomas Romney (94/130).

84 Sideboard table, dated 17.11.1787, for Dr. Crompton of Derby, no. 5938; made by John Savage, the corner pieces shaded by T. Romney. A note states that a similar one was made for Mr. W. Adams, Pottery, Staffs., no. 6369, 7'2" long, by Thomas Smith, in April 1788; H 3'1" × 7' × 2'6½" (94/144).

85 Sideboard table, dated 14.9.1787; mahogany, the top crossbanded with king-wood, and with shaded stringing, the front edge banded with purplewood and strung, the front rail banded with blue veneers and strung white; made by James Burton, carved by Henry Gibson (94/98).

86 Sideboard table, [April–May 1794] for William Wilson Carus, Esq., no. 30,692; H 3'0½" × 7'2" × 3'0½"; made by William Beckett, turned by D. Ball, carved by Gibson (96/1081).

87 Sideboard table, dated 14.5.1787, for Miss Rawlinson, no. 3132; 6'10" long, with cabled legs and carved capitals (94/1).

88 'Circular' sideboard, dated 28.9.1787, for Miss Shepherd of Kirkham, Lancs., no. 4545; H 2'10" × 6'6" × 3'0½"; shaded stringing and plain stringing, purplewood and kingwood bands on the top and front; made by Richard Slater, helped by William Beckett, the two cornerpieces shaded by Thomas Romney (94/110).

89 Sideboard table, dated 31.3.1789, for S. Jones, Esq., no. 9884; mahogany, with purplewood bands and shaded stringing; H 3' × 6'11" × 2'9"; made by C. Procter, carved by Mr. Gibson (95/485).

90 Sideboard table, 1788, for John Christian, Esq. (735/1, f.56v).

91 Sideboard table, dated 19.9.1797, for Robert Peel, Esq., of Drayton Manor, Staffs.; mahogany; H 36½" × 7'6½" × 3'2"/2'9"; made by S. Cooper (97/1382).

92 Sideboard table, dated 26.6.1799, ordered by the London shop for Mr. Fielding of Catterall, Lancs., no. 68,127; mahogany, the top edge crossbanded with black rosewood, all the rails banded with rosewood; angles, band, and two strings on the bottom of the rails; turned and cabled legs; the brass rod supplied from London; made by Samuel Cooper (98/1535).

93 Sideboard table, dated 27.11.1786, for Thomas Withington Jun. of Pendleton, Manchester; five term legs, four in front, each fluted on three sides (36 flutes in all), top of legs with three strings, panelled; one of end drawers lined with lead, the other having mahogany partitioning, the middle drawers plain; made by John Savage (93/454).

94 Sideboard table, dated 5.9.1788, for

Mr. George Phillips, no. 9124; shaded stringing on the edge of the top and two white angles. A purplewood longband round the circular (i.e. curved) drawers and shaded stringing, the inside divided for bottles, the tablet crossbanded with tulipwood and strung, the appearance of a drawer each side of ditto, longbanded with purplewood and white strings, the top of the legs crossbanded with tulipwood and a white string in the side of ditto, fifty-two flutes in the legs; made by William Nailor (94/394).

95   Sideboard table, dated 2.9.1788, for T. Unsworth Esq. (see note 36); 'very handsome', the rails all longbanded with purplewood and strung, a shaded string on the edge of the top and two white angles, astragal on the bottom of the rail broken over the legs, four front legs carved on three sides, two back legs on two sides, six paterae carved from the solid, the top overhanging by one inch at the front and two inches at the back; carved tablet from London 'very richly wrought' with drapery, oakleaves, ribbons, vase, &c.; sixteen sides of the legs carved with plain husks in sunk panels and raffle leaves above; made by H. Walling, carved by Bayley; H 35⅛" × 7' × 3' (94/386).

96   Sideboard table, dated 27.2.1799, for the Earl of Eglinton; mahogany, with white string, no. 37,593; the legs termed and sunk in hollow panels and richly carved on fourteen sides, the tablet also richly carved; made by Isaac Robinson, legs and tablet carved by John Ford, varnished by Thomas Romney (98/1507).

97   Sideboard table, dated 21.11.1794, for Daniel Leo, Esq., of Llanerch Park, St. Asaph, no. 31,490; mahogany, the front edge of the top crossbanded and with two angles, the spandrels longbanded and strung, a broad longband and string round all drawers; the tablet centrematched and longbanded with kingwood, the legs sunk in panels; made by R. Clarkson, carved by Gibson (96/1135).

98   Sideboard table, dated 25.5.1799, for Samuel Joseph, Esq., no. 67,813; mahogany, the six front legs panelled with canarywood on three sides, the two back legs

ditto on one side; the drawer fronts and cupboard doors with white angles and panelled with a small band of purplewood and a small white string on each side; the top crossbanded on the edge; H 3' × 7'4½" × 16¾"; made by Thomas Darwen (98/1532).

99   Sideboard table, dated 27.10.1789, for the Rev. Mr. Hudson, no. 10,896; mahogany; H 3' 0½" × 5' 4½" × 2'7"; made by J. Hessledon (95/542).

100   Chest of drawers night table, dated 25.5.1797; H 2'6½" (when closed); (97/1348).

101   Bedstep night table, dated 10.1.1799, for the Earl of Eglinton, no. 27,615; mahogany and cedar; H 35" × 28" × 22"; made by Samuel Cooper (98/1492).

102   Semicircular night table, June 1789, sent to the London shop; deal, made by R. Clarkson (95/507).

103   Pair of bed pillars, [about December 1767], for Mr. Starkey at Carlisle; gothic frets; made by J. Dowbiggin and '2 lads' (90/71).

104   Bedstead, dated 25.3.1788, for Mrs. John Christian of Workington Hall, Cumberland; elliptical cornice, mahogany footposts carved by H. Gibson, except the feathers and vases which were carved in London; H 8'6" × 5'6" × 6'6" (94/268).

105   Bedstead, dated 5.8.1788; mahogany footposts, carved and painted cornice; pillar H 8'0½" + cornice 5" and 6" × 5'2½" × 6'6"; subsidiary woods = Danzig oak and deal; made by John Crowdson (94/354).

106   Bedstead, dated July 1789, for William Egerton, Esq., of Tatton Park, Cheshire, no. 10,513; H 8'8" × 6'1" × 6'1"; bedstead made by J. Atkinson, cornices by J. Mally (95/511).

107   Bedstead, dated 20.2.1799, for the Earl of Eglinton (family bedroom at Eglinton Castle, Ayrshire); mahogany, octagon pedestals, pillars H 10' × 6' × 7'1"; pillars turned, cabled, and carved by John Kilner, cornice painted by J. Atkinson; made by John Mally, varnished by Thomas Romney (98/1506).

108 Couch bed with canopy, dated 10.7. 1788, for Mrs. John Christian; made by J.Slater, the canopy by J.Malley (94/342).

109 Couch bed with canopy, undated but about 1790; note the turned vases at the angles (735/1, f.118).

110 Press-bed, 1771, for 'Lawyer' [Thomas] Barrow; mahogany and deal; fret, cut cornice, and carved shield in pediment; made by William Townley and W. Charles (? Chailor) (90/172).

111 Bason stand ('common') [May 1760] with shelf below (89/17).

112 Shaving stand, dated 15.9.1787; H 2'10¼" × 16"; shelf below (94/104).

113 Corner washing stand, dated 20.3. 1797, shelf below (97/1325).

114 Chest of drawers ('common size') [May 1787]; H 2'9½" × 3'6" × 19" (94/6).

115 Chest of drawers, dated 19.12.1789, for the London shop no. 12,265; satinwood, framed back, a black longband round the top and white angles, ditto round all the drawers and part of the ends, nine black flutes in each pillar, the feet fluted with black; H 2'9" × 3'9½" × 24½"; made by Isaac Hesseldon (95/554).

116 'A commode with toilet', dated 20.5. 1799 (98/1530, but this version taken from 735/1, f.92v).

117 Commode, dated 3.11.1789, for the London shop, no. 11,108; mahogany, two white angles round the edge of the top; a slide on the top drawers covered with green cloth; framed back; the fronts veneered with upright 'birchings'; H 2'10½" × 3'9½" × 21" (95/545).

118 Commode, dated 24.10.1789, for the London shop, no. 11,122; satinwood, top all crossbanded with tulipwood, all drawers ditto plus a white margin; partitions all

banded with purplewood, also the ends; edge of top crossbanded with kingwood, plus white angles; H 3'0½" × 3'9" × 17"; made by Cooper (95/540).

119 Commode (also called 'cupboard'), dated 4.10.1797, for John Clifton, Esq., of Lytham Hall, Lancs.; satinwood, the two end panels and doors with a broad black band and a small white string round, then panelled with the same to represent panels and framing, the four pilasters crossbanded with tulipwood and with black angles; the doors (not shown) finished as the other two panels; H 2'6" × 3'3" × 18"; made by P.Briscoe (97/1385).

120 Commode ('circular cupboard, say commode'), dated 9.12.1787, for John Trafford, Esq. of Trafford Park, Lancs.; satinwood, banded with purplewood, kingwood, &c., H 2'9½" × 3'6" diameter × 23¼"; made by Peter Brisco (94/178).

121 Commode (one of a pair), dated 18.6.1788, for Sir Roger Newdigate of Arbury Hall, Warwickshire; mahogany, with purplewood crossbanding, shaded stringing, white stringing, &c., plus two inlaid ovals and an inlaid shell (for full description see my article cited in note 12 to the Introduction); H 2'9¼" × 5'0¼" × 2'; one made by S.Cooper, the other by J. Savage (94/320, but this version taken from 735/1, f.69v).

122 Commode, dated 29.7.1789, no. 10,646; satinwood, inlaid with blue strings in the pilasters, black corners on the legs, and kingwood on the feet, the doors feather-banded; H 4'6" × 3'6" × 6½/14"; a virtually identical piece was called a 'sheveret' in the Tatton Park commission — see note 10 to Introduction; made by J. Burton (95/513).

123 Commode, dated 4.11.1790, for the Rev. Francis Annesley via the London shop, no. 14,547; mahogany plus 'birching' veneers on oak; white and black ebony banding and angles; baywood shelves and drawers; made by John Savage (95/669).

124 Cabinet [about May 1768] for Mr. Roger Hesketh; made by Edmund, John Park, William Lupton, Joseph, and James Townson (90/89).

125 Plate case, dated 20.12.1770, for Mr. William Sudell; made by Christopher Dixon, Thomas Wilson, and John Turner; H 6'5½" × 3'5" (90/162, inserted leaf).

126 Cabinet, dated 24.11.1788, for Mrs. Daniel Wilson of Dallam Tower, Westmorland; whitewood, for painting; made by Robinson and King (94/444).

127 Cabinet, dated 18.9.1793, no. 19,949; mahogany and purplewood; the lower part made by Robert Fell; the upper part made, turned, painted, and varnished by Thomas Romney; the 'cupola' enriched with carved and gilt capitals, and 'birching' veneers on the door; the form suggests a religious purpose, e.g. to enclose a crucifix or statuette (96/1010).

128 Hexagon cabinet to contain a shell-work temple; dated 26.1.1795, for Mrs. Quincey, Manchester, no. 31,558; mahogany, painted; made by Thomas Romney (97/1144).

129 Low wardrobe with writing drawer, dated 25.6.1788; note the 'sliding prospect' in the centre of the the interior of the drawer, also the characteristically Gillow ogee feet; H 3'7¼" × 4' × 23"; made by Thomas Whiteingdale (94/332).

130 Low wardrobe [September 1793] for Mr. Sanderson; mahogany, with satinwood oval panels inlaid in the writing drawer; H 3'8½" × 3'11½" × 23½"; made by T. Lister (96/1009).

131 Clothes press [April] 1759, for Mr. Addison (89/23).

132 Cabinet or bureau-wardrobe, dated 27.2.1788, ordered by Mrs. Wilson in [Queen] Square [Lancaster] for Mrs. Gibson, no. 6169; mahogany, with 'birching' veneers on the panels and fronts; deal and oak in the drawers; bottom part made by Crookall, top part by Thomas Smith, with further work by Thomas Romney and William Briscoe on the writing drawer (94/246).

133 'A large piece of furniture', April 1766, for John France, Esq., of Rawcliffe Hall, Lancs.; mahogany, cedar, and oak;

note the cresting, frieze, rococo borders of the fielded panels, and swelled ogee feet; made by William Lupton, William Taylor, William Askew, John Serjeant, and Joseph Foster (90/11).

134 Secretary and bookcase, dated 21.7.1787, no. 4265; called bureau-bookcase in the Waste Book (94/54).

135 Wardrobe with a writing-drawer, dated 25.3.1788; mahogany, oak, and deal; H 7'1½" × 4'1" × 24/23" (94/266).

136 Wardrobe, dated 19.3.1799, for the Earl of Eglinton's dressing-room at Eglinton Castle, Ayrshire; mahogany, oak, deal, and cedar; the centre top having four sliding boxes and eight grooves, the bottom four plain drawers; the left wing lined with green baize, the right having twenty-five grooves and six sliding shelves; H 7' × 6' × 21½", the breakfront centre projecting 2¼"; made by William Stubbs (98/1514).

137 Desk and bookcase, [January 1771]; Thomas Wilson made the desk, William Lupton the remainder; the inscription notes '6 drawers of equal Length in the Bottom 5 Inches deep', but 7 are indicated on the sketch, notably the characteristic triple drawer arrangement at the top; although the sketch is rough, it indicates an enriched cornice, carved roses in the 'hollow corners' of the panel mouldings, and double pilasters with frets on either side of the centre cupboard in the desk (90/167).

138 Bureau and bookcase, dated June 1771, for Atherton Gwyllim, Esq.; the two top 'drawers' are sham, with a writing drawer behind; note the carved frieze, carved roses in the 'hollow corners' of the panel mouldings, and the swelled ogee feet; lower part H 3'0½"; upper part H 3' (90/177).

139 Bureau and bookcase with a writing drawer, dated 25.5.1788, for John Haworth of Manchester, no. 6523; mahogany, oak, and deal, with kingwood crossband and plain string of holly; H 7'0½" × 4' ×25/13¼"; made by Isaac Hazleton, drawers lettered by Thomas Romney (94/312).

140 Bureau and bookcase, dated 12.8.1796, for Ralph Lodge, Esq., Carlisle; mahogany, the lettered covers banded with canarywood; H 9' 4" × 4'5" × 23"; made by John Hodgson (97/1260).

141 Writing desk with sliding prospect, [June–July] 1787; mahogany, H 3'3½" × 4' × 22"; feet 5", drawers 7", 6", 5", 4"; note the triple drawers in the top row (94/48).

142 Desk interiors, with prices for workmanship, 1792; note the pilasters (single in nos. 3 and 5, double in nos. 4,6,7,8), and sliding prospects or tills in nos. 7 and 8 (67/83).

143 Twelve designs for bookcase doors, dated 1792 (67/168).

144 Secretaire-bookcase, dated 10.11.1786, for Lady Clifford of Chudleigh, via the London shop no. 2222; satinwood, the backs and shelves of deal, the shelves edged with satinwood, the satinwood doors and partitions all crossbanded with black rosewood, the ends also crossbanded; the drawer fronts all with blue longbands ⅜" broad, with white strings instead of beads; three inlaid paterae in the frieze; from the floor to the underside of the desk drawer = 30"; the desk drawer, which appears as two, = 10" deep; made by W. Beckett (93/443).

145 Secretary and bookcase, dated 5.5.1788, no. 6172; satinwood and purplewood veneers on deal and oak; H 3'6"/4'4" × 3'3" × 20/11"; made by Thomas Atkinson except the writing drawer by Richard Gibson (94/173).

146 Secretaire and bookcase, dated 19.7.1794, for the London shop; made by R. Clarkson (96/1102).

147 Secretaire and bookcase, dated 30.6.1792, for John Barnaby, Esq.; satinwood, the 'tower corners' (columns) inlaid with purplewood bands, 8 flutes in each column, columns 1⅝" diameter, the panels banded with purplewood; lozenge doors, the 'guts' (glazing-bars) veneered with purplewood with a white string on each side; oval ivory escutcheons with a black string round; 'grass green' curtains; ink and sand bottles in desk drawer; 3' wide; made by John Shaw (96/866).

148 Secretaire and bookcase, dated 18.10.1797, for William Johnson, land surveyor, no. 36,400; new cove cornice; H 7'1½" × 3'6¼" × 14½/20½"; made by J. Hodgson (97/1390).

149 Secretaire on legs, dated 19.8.1788, for Miss Oliver of Preston; mahogany, the top and sides solid, the bottom veneered on oak, the interior drawers crossbanded; H 29¾" + 4" + 5" + 2'10 + 1¾" × 2'9½" × 18/11½"; the bookcase made by Thomas Atkinson (94/212).

150 Sheveret, dated 5.7.1790, for the London shop, no. 13,014; satinwood, the outer edges crossbanded with tulipwood, and white strings and black and white next the satinwood; the drawer in the bottom part with a blue string on the outer edge of the crossband; a white band with two blue edges on the bottom of the rail ¼" wide; H 29¼" + 10½" × 21½" × 14"; made by S. Cooper (95/603).

151 Writing table and bookshelf, dated 13.2.1796, for Mr. Hesketh of Wennington Hall, Lancs.; mahogany, H 32½"/29⅞" × 2'9⅞" × 18⅛/10½/8⅞"; made by R. Townson (97/1227).

152 Secretaire, dated 12.4.1798, no. 36,991; H 3'6¼" × 3'4" × 19¾" made by James Burton (97/1436).

153 Writing desk (also called French secretaire), dated 8.9.1789, for the London shop; satinwood, ebony stringing and banding, kingwood banding round oval panel; H 5'2" × 3" × 14¾"; made by Thomas Smith, James Burton, and Robert Clarkson (95/521). See also Colour Plate 10.

154 Secretaire and little bookcase, dated 3.6.1790, for the London shop, no. 12,597; satinwood, with white bands round the edge of the drawers in lieu of beads, the outside banded with ebony; the top banded with ebony (shelf, bottom, and scrolls); two little prospect doors at each end, two little drawers in the right hand, the other quite open, the ovals veneered with fine wood; H 3'6¼" + 12" + 7⅛" × 2'9¾" × 16¾"; the top made by S. Cooper (95/604).

155 Secretaire and bookshelf, dated 28.6.1798, ordered by the London shop for the Countess of Derby at Knowsley Hall, Lancs., no. 37,242; satinwood, the top solid with a purplewood crossband on the edges and a small black and white string on each angle; the cupboard doors with an oval of fine satinwood 'birching' and a purplewood band and string round; the bottom part drawer front veneered with fine satinwood, banded with purplewood and strung; the cupboard door panels veneered centre-matched and strung; the framing with a black moulding banded and strung; the 'towers' inlaid wth purplewood to represent flutes; made by T. Drape, James Burton Senior, and William Stubbs (97/1456).

156 Bookcase, dated 5.3.1788, for Mr. Ainsworth near Bolton le Moors, Lancs.; there was no base; mahogany; H 3'10" × 3'3" × 13"; made by William Getskell (94/250).

157 Bookcase, dated 4.2.1788, for Mrs. Leigh of Leigh Place, Wigan, Lancs.; the late use of walnut was owing to the re-use of old doors; H 8' × 3'4"/2'11½" × 19/14"; made by Isaac Robinson (94/226).

158 Bookcase, dated 5.10.1790, for Mr. Tyrrell; no base — cf. no. 156 (95/661).

159 Hanging bookcase, dated 21.11.1797, for Thomas Green, Esq., no. 36,549; mahogany, with wire panels; H 4'6" × 3'9½" × 8¼"; made by Robert Townson (97/1401).

160 Bookshelf with drawer, dated 8.4.1788, for Charles Gibson of Myers-cough House, Garstang, Lancs.; mahogany and oak; H 3'7" × 2'6" × 9½"; made by Isaac Robinson (94/270).

161 Bookshelf, dated 31.12.1788, for John Christian, Esq., of Workington Hall, Cumberland, no. 1964; mahogany, with brass rod and green silk curtains; H 2'8" + 6½" pediment × 3'8¾" × 7"; made by T. Atkinson (94/462).

162 'Moving library', December 1794, sent to the London shop; mahogany, all solid, all edges long-banded with purple-wood and white angles; H 3'0½" × 22" × 9⅞/7¾"; made by William Swan (96/1136).

163 Black and gold frame or table for a marble slab, dated 17.9.1796, for Daniel Wilson, Esq., of Dallam Tower, Westmorland; mahogany, deal, and limewood; H 34½" × 3'7" × 16"; drawing out and part making by T. Romney, capitals carved by Gibson, finishing by B. Townson, black ground, gilding, and fluting by Ford (97/1276).

164 Small library bookcase, [July 1766], for Mr. Thomas Park of Liverpool; the lower part the same as a clothes press (90/25).

165 Library bookcase and wardrobe, [April 1789], for Mr. John Philips, Norfolk Street, Manchester, no. 9919; joinery by J. Croudson, J. Wilson, and Robert Green-wood; cabinet work by Isaac Robinson and Robert Clarkson (95/490,673).

166 Library bookcase, [May 1787], for stock; a writing drawer in the centre of the lower part with sliding boxes for clothes under, the left-hand end with more sliding boxes and one drawer above, the right-hand end with drawers only; H 9' × 8'2" × 22/14½" (94/8).

167 Library bookcase, dated 8.8.1792, for Lady Wakes via the London shop; wire panels, circular panels of best rosewood below, the pediment of handsome curled 'birching' veneer, no fan; H 9' × 9'2"; made by W. Nailor, John Cape, John Crookall, and R. Savage; William Moore framed the bottom of the back (96/883).

168 Library bookcase, dated 15.7.1797, for Mr. Stainbank; the pediments with fine centrematched 'birching' veneers, the top flat ditto with a band of purplewood and a white string round the outside; the bottom panels with fine 'birching' veneer and cross-band; Tuscan cornice; the top in three parts, also the bottom, connected by the top flat, cornice, and pediments in one piece; made by S. Bryan and J. Fell (97/1361).

169 Library bookcase, March 1792, for the Bishop of Llandaff; mahogany, made by R. Townson, H. Walker, J. Malley, and R. Scott (96/835).

170 Gothic library bookcase, dated 24.7.1795, for Daniel Leo, Esq., of Llanerch Park, St. Asaph; deal, japanned blue ground and ornaments to match his drawing room chairs; H 9'8" × 12'6"; made by Townson, Scott, Walker, Harker; Thomas Romney made the pediment and battlements, fixed the mouldings, and made the fret work (97/1185).

171 Gothic screen, dated 5.2.1798, made for the Butler chapel in St. Michael's Church, St. Michael's-on-Wyre, Lancs. [destroyed]; deal and limewood, carved by John Ford (97/1417).

172 Buffet, dated 4.8.1787; H 6" + 2'2½" + 4'8" (94/70).

173 Corner cupboard, [May–June, 1787], with pitched pediment; mahogany, H 3'6" (without pediment) × 25½" × 4¼" (94/22).

174 Buffet, dated 29.5.1798, for Mr. Burrow, no. 37,216; good dentil cornice, crossbanded frieze, pilasters fluted at the top and cabled below, bottom doors with a small astragal and crossbanded margin, panels veneered with fine mahogany 'birchings'; interior painted and gilded; made by William Gatskill (97/1450).

175 Corner cupboard for clothes, dated 6.8.1787, no. 4460; H 6' (94/72).

176 Tub on pedestal, 1767, for Philip Howard, Esq., of Corby Castle, Cumberland; setting out by John Neiel, making by John Pendleton, four festoons carved by T. Pedestal 24½" high (90/43).

177 Cistern, dated 6.5.1767, for Mr. [Philip] Howard, of Corby Castle, Cumberland, 'something like Mr. Saul's with 3 hoops & 2 faced handles', the brass hoops from London (90/43).

178 Cistern, dated 28.12.1787, for Mr. Trafford of Trafford Park, Lancs.;

mahogany on oak; H 11¾" + 2" + 8½" × 27" × 20½"; made by John Wilson, legs carved by Williams, fluting by T. Romney, legs turned by D. Ball; lined with lead (94/200).

179 Oval cistern, dated 6.4.1799, for the Earl of Eglinton, no. 37,597; mahogany, with black and white stringing, tops of legs with hollow panels enriched with a drop of leaves, legs termed and sunk in panels on three sides each; lined with patent copper; made by John Savage, carving and panelling by Clement Gibson (98/1516).

180 Octagon 'temporary cellar' or gardevine (= garde du vin), [Sept. 1769], for Mr. Sunderland Junr. (90/125).

181 Gardevine, [about January 1768], for the Rev. W. Harris at Prestwich, Lancs. (90/75).

182 Gardevine, dated 8.11.1788, for John Christian of Workington Hall, Cumberland; mahogany, ovals in top and front crossbanded with kingwood, with purplewood longband and shading within round the outside, purplewood longband round the cants, ends, and back, and white stringing; sunk panels on three sides of each leg; H 28½" × 18⅛" × 14⅝"; made by John Dixson, carved by H. Gibson (94/440).

183 Gardevine, [May–June 1787], with trunk lid, to hold six bottles; H 2'5" × 16¾" × 13" (94/24).

184 Round tub on a pedestal, dated 26.10.1790, for Sir John Leicester via the London shop, no. 14,068; made by John Wilson (95/668).

185 Knife box and plate basket, dated 25.7.1794, for the Wareroom; made by T. Romney (96/1104).

186 Dumb waiters, dated 14.12.1787; mahogany (94/180).

187 Vase, dated 20.6.1788; deal, mahogany, 'birching' veneer, plain blue and white string; plated handles, with astragal hoops, rams' heads, and a flame on top; turned by Duke Ball, carved by Mr.

Williams, varnished by James Ripley, made by Samuel Cooper (94/1972).

188 Vase knife case, dated 27.9.1796, for Shakespeare Phillips, Manchester; mahogany, made by Charles Lupton, carved by H. Gibson (97/1278).

189 Vase and pedestal, [May–June 1787], for Sir James Ibbetson of Denton Hall, Yorks., no. 1983; pedestal H 3'0½" × 16½"; vase H 6¼" + 15¾" + 9"; inlaying and engraving by John Dowbiggin (94/34).

190 Vase knife case to stand on a pedestal (one of a pair), dated 21.8.1792, for Sir Walter Blount of Mawley Hall, Salop, no. 17,817; one made by S. Cooper, the frieze carved by H. Gibson; annotated 'should be a square astragal panel instead of oval' (96/892).

191 Vase and pedestal, undated, about 1788 (cf. Fig. 192) (735/1, f.66).

192 Vase and pedestal, dated 23.9.1788, for John Christian of Workington Hall, Cumberland, no. 8012; scale 1½" to 1' (94/406).

193 'Union set' (dressing glass on base with three drawers), [August 1759] (89/4).

194 Swing glass, dated 26.6.1788, with two brass spires; made by Isaac Robinson (94/334).

195 Commode box and pillar for an oval glass, dated 30.3.1797; satinwood (97/1331).

196 Frame for a glass, dated 18.1.1790, no. 12,280; limewood, made by T. Romney (95/558).

197 Pier glass frame (one of a pair), January 1771, for Mr. Crozier of Antigua; carved and gilt 'pretty Neatly' (90/164).

198 Pier glass frame, dated 4.8.1790, for Messrs. John Barrow and Sons, made by 'Jonathan' [? Harker] (95/639).

199 Two pier glass frames, dated 3.8.1797, (97/1369).

200 Pier giass frame, dated 6.8.1788; mahogany, varnished and part gilt; H 5'10", glass 21" × 2'6"; gilding and varnishing by J. Dowbiggin (94/360).

201 Pier glass frame, dated 24.9.1798, for John Upton, Esq.; made by John Mally, gilded by John Ford (98/1475b).

202 Girandoles, undated but about 1790/95; yellow and grey wash (735/1, f.87).

203 Girandole and wall decoration or surmount; undated but about 1790/1800 (735/1, f.90).

204 Gilt overmantel glass for a drawing room, for Thornton, dated 14.12.1792 (96/924).

205 Pier glass, undated but about 1790; yellow wash (735/1, f.100).

206 Decorative surmount (probably for a pier glass), undated but about 1790; yellow wash (735/1, f.113).

207 Pier glass, undated but about 1790; yellow wash (735/1, f.98).

208 Decorative surmount (? for pier glass or window cornice), undated, about 1790/95; yellow wash (735/1, f.102).

209 Pier glass and table, undated but about 1790; yellow wash (735/1, f.104).

210 Girandoles, undated but about 1790/95; yellow wash (735/1, f.94).

211 Pier glass, undated, but about 1790; yellow wash (735/1, f.99).

212 Girandoles, undated but about 1790/95; yellow wash (735/1, f.92).

213 Pier glass frame (one of a pair), dated 19.2.1799, for Sir Henry Hoghton of Walton Hall, Lancs.; made by John Middleton and Jos Lambert, the ornaments by Robert Townson; carved and smoothed by John Ford; gilded by Mrs. John Ford; plate fitted and blocked by Richard Leeming (98/1505).

214 Pier glass, dated 20.1.1794, for the showroom; white and gold, plate 50" × 30"; made, carved, and gilded by Dobson (96/1044).

215 Girandole, undated but about 1790/95 (735/1, f.90v).

216 Chimney glass, undated but about 1790/95; yellow wash (735/1, f.104v).

217 Tripod candlestand, undated but about 1790/95 (735/1, f.95).

218 Girandole, undated but about 1790; yellow wash (735/1, f.88).

219 Girandole, undated but about 1790/95; yellow wash (735/1, f.91).

220 Girandole, undated but about 1790; yellow wash (735/1, f.91).

221 Girandole, undated but about 1790/95; yellow wash (735/1, f.93).

222 Two oval firescreens on tripod bases, with a decorative festoon superimposed; undated, but about 1785/95; yellow and blue wash (735/1, f.107).

223 Oval firescreen on tripod base, June 1787; H 5' (94/36).

224 Firescreen on triangular base, dated 26.7.1796, for the Earl of Strafford at Wentworth Castle, Yorks.; japanned blue ground, with green strokes and ornaments; made by D. Ball, japanner unknown (97/1254).

225 Oval firescreen on tripod base, dated 30.9.1788, for John Christian at Belle Isle, Westmorland, no. 7093; satinwood, made by Samuel Cooper, complete with fluted pillar, for the dressing-room; tapestry on one side and client's damask on the other (94/414).

226 Firescreen, December 1788, (one of three), for John Christian; mahogany; made by S. Cooper, and carved by H. Gibson; 'our damask one side, your tapestry the other' (94/456).

227 Window cornice (one of three), February 1787, for the drawing-room of Standish Hall, Lancs.; a medallion of Diana in the oval; made by John Mally and carved by Gibson (93/497).

228 Window cornice, dated 3.9.1795, for Sir Henry Philip Hoghton at Walton Hall, Lancs.; deal, made by John Malley, painted in a gothic design by James Hutton (97/1193).

229 Window cornice, dated 17.9.1789, for Samuel Jones, Esq.; made by John Malley, japanned by Knight, carved by Gibson (95/526).

230 Window cornice and reefed curtain, undated but about 1790; brown and green wash (735/1, f.130).

231 Window cornice, the tablet ornamented with Diana and the stag, with reefed curtain; undated, but about 1790; yellow and pink wash (735/1, f.129).

232 Music or reading stand, [about 1766–67], made by William Lupton (90/41).

233 Reading stand, dated 23.8.1792; mahogany; supplied from London for the Bishop of Llandaff (96/893).

234 Flower stand, dated 15.9.1788, for Alan Chambre, Esq., of Abbot Hall, Kendal, Westmorland; japanned (94/398).

235 What-not, dated 22.3.1790, for the showroom; mahogany, made by John Savage (95/579).

236 Picture frame, [about December 1767], for Mr. Strickland (90/70).

237 Bracket (one of a pair), dated 21.11.1797, for Edward Suart, no. 36,540; burnished gold; made by John Ford (97/1401).

238 Tea chest, dated 15.3.1798, for Lady Hoghton of Walton Hall, Lancs., no. 36,772; a black string at each angle and a broad black band at the base; three silver canisters, also handle, feet, and escutcheon; made by T. Romney (97/1430).

239 Canterbury, undated but apparently for Sir John Shaw Stewart of Ardgowan, Renfrewshire, and therefore 1799/1802 (735/1, f.71).

240 Oval tea tray, [April 1790], for Mr. Feilden, Blackburn; satinwood, 30" × 21" (95/594).

241 Oval tea tray, [November] 1791; satinwood, veneered with blue and green; a crossband in the centre and close to the rim; indented edge; two black bands and one white band on the edge, plated handles; lined with green baize; made by John Wilson (95/798).

242 A 'French' armchair, [about March 1761], for Mr. Bell's dining-room [at Thirsk Hall, Yorks.], with fluted 'feet' (i.e. legs) and carved elbows; alternatively with 'commode' (i.e. curved) front; frets, and brackets (89/47).

243 Settee [about March 1761], for Mr. Dowker of Kendal, Westmorland; carved splats and legs (89/39).

244 Smoking chair, dated 30.11.1787; H 2'6", seat 19" × 19" (94/162).

245 The 'old splat back' chair with horizontal pierced splats, straight seat rails, plain square legs, and low stretchers (67/68).

246 Reading chair, dated 5.8.1794, for Mr. A. Cottam of Clerk Hill, Whalley, Lancs.; mahogany; made by J. Savage, caned by R. Francis, candlestands by T. Romney (96/1109).

247 Chair with horizontal pierced splats, [December 1769], for Captain Hazell; walnut, the front legs shaped with some resemblance to bamboo; cf. Fig. 245 (90/130).

248 The 'three upright baluster splats' chair, common straight seat with plain tapered legs (67/67).

249 Carved splat back chair, undated but about 1780/90 (735/1, f.10).

250 The 'new fanback' chair (735/1, f.8).

251 Fan back chair with arched top rail and plain square legs (67/66).

252 Chair with pierced upright splat, dated 22.1.1799, for the Rev. R. Hudson no. 67,715; mahogany, made by John Savage (98/1498).

253 Hall chair, dated 1.3.1786, for Samuel Hibbert, Esq., of Manchester; made by John Dowbiggin and carved by Henry Gibson (93/309).

254 Hall chair, 1788 [for Stephen Tempest, Esq., Broughton Hall, Yorks.] (735/1, f.22).

255 Hall chair, undated, but about 1790 (735/1, f.22).

256 Gothic armchair, October 1799, for John France, Esq., [of Rawcliffe Hall, Lancs.]; made by John Harrison and japanned by John Atkinson (98/1546).

257 Gothic arch chair, November 1784, intended to have a green leather seat; carved by Williams (93/128).

258 Chair, undated but 1794, [for Daniel Wilson, Esq., of Dallam Tower, Westmorland]; beech, simulating bamboo (735/1, f.41v).

259 Chair, undated but about 1790: 'a China chair' with plain square legs/tapered legs/ and folding seat (67/63v).

260 'A camel back stay rail' chair, with straight side rails, low stretchers and plain tapered legs/fluted legs and a second back rail (67/63).

261 Shield-back chair with carved splat, undated but about 1785/90 (67/65).

262 Shield-back chair with horizontal splats, undated but about 1785/90 (67/66v).

263 A 'dog-leg splat' chair with no holes in the splats, straight side rails, plain tapered legs and low stretchers/alternatively two holes in the middle splat and fluted legs; undated but about 1785/90 (67/64v).

264 The 'old balloon' back chair, introduced in 1785 (735/1, f.9).

265 The 'new balloon' back chair, introduced in 1786 (735/1, f.10).

266 Cabriole armchair, undated but about 1790 (735/1, f.41).

267 Cabriole armchair, dated 25.10.1786, for Robert Peel, Esq., no. 1863; whitewood, painted, with damask cover; H 3' × 19⅜" (seat)/16¾" (back); carved by H. Gibson (93/435).

268 Oval-back chair with 'honeysuckle' splat; undated, but about 1785/90 (67/71).

269 The 'new Catherine wheel' chair with arms and swept side rails and front rail, plain tapered legs and no stretchers (67/72).

270 Armchair, undated but about 1790; green wash (735/1, f.17).

271 Oval-back chair with carved splats, undated but about 1780/90 (735/1, f.9).

272 Heart-shaped back chair, carved with wheatears, dated 9.10.1788 [for the dining room at Workington Hall, Cumberland], no. 8015; made by John Savage (94/416).

273 Elbow chair, 'Feather Back' [usually called 'drapery and feather'] dated 19.1.1788, for N. Crompton, Esq., Manchester; H 17¼" + 2⅛" + 22" × 22" (at front) × 19" deep; mahogany with beech seat; made by John Kilner and carved by H. Gibson; annotated 'mahogany seat rails hollow in length & crooked side rails, which makes a good deal of waste' (94/212).

274 Armchair, dated 30.7.1789, for John Trafford, Esq., of Trafford Park, Lancs. (95/514, but this version taken from 735/1, f.14).

275 Wyatt's pattern chair (first mentioned in 1782) dated 1791 (95/697, but this version taken from 735/1, f.12).

276 A mahogany chair with three upright splats, dated 11.2.1791 (95/697, but this version taken from 735/1, f.10).

277 Shield-shaped-back chair with carved splats, undated but about 1785/90 (735/1, f.12).

278 Dining chair, dated 30.9.1793, for Shakespeare Phillips; mahogany, made by John Savage (96/1018).

279 Spanish-back chair, dated 23.12.1789 (95/555, but this version taken from 735/1, f.13).

280 Lozenge-back armchair, dated 21.11.1792, no. 18,523; japanned; H 16⅝" + 17" × 23" at front (96/916).

281 Cabriole armchair, dated 29.10.1788, for John Christian, Esq. (for a dressing room at Workington Hall, Cumberland); made by Lupton and Milner, carved by T. Romney; whitewood, japanned white and green (94/432).

282 Chair with carved splats, probably for a dining-room, undated but about 1790 (735/1, f.17).

283 Chair with plain splats, probably for a dining-room, undated but about 1790 (735/1, f.17).

284 Armchair, square back, undated but about 1790; green wash (735/1, f.39).

285 Armchair, square back, undated but about 1790 (735/1, f.39).

286 Tablet top-rail chair, dated 24.8.1797, for Robert Peel, Esq.; satinwood veneer and string; made by John Savage (97/1377).

287 Chair, dated 24.7.1799, for Edward Lloyd Esq., of Penlyan near Wrexham, Denbighshire; brass moulding on the seat rail; covered in red morocco; made by John Savage (98/1537).

288 Armchair, undated but about 1790; green wash (735/1, f.19).

289 Sofa, dated 31.10.1786, for Robert Peel, Esq.; carved leaves on the stump (i.e. arms), cabled legs &c., no. 1864; made by R. Slater, carved by Henry Gibson, and painted by J. Ripley. Gillows referred to this as the French or cabriole style sofa, i.e. with late rococo curves, scrolls, &c. (93/440).

290 Small sofa, dated 18.8.1787, for Mrs. Henry Rawlinson; 'circular', i.e. curved, back; beech, painted; legs 14" high, H to elbow 2' + 17½" to centre of back × 4'8" long × seat 2' deep; made by Richard Slater, legs turned by Duke Ball; painted by Thomas Romney, who also made the pattern (94/82).

291 Duchesse, comprising two armchairs and a stool, September 1793, for Daniel Leo, Esq., of Llanerch Park, St. Asaph, Flint.; covered in red leather (96/1017).

292 Stool, dated 26.10.1786, for Robert Peel, Esq., no. 1864; covered in blue damask; H 29" × 4'2½" × 14" (93/436).

293 Sofa, May 1791, for Mr. Drinkwater, no. 15,892; mahogany and beech; made by R. Slater and carved by H. Gibson. Gillows referred to this as the English style sofa (95/723). See also Colour Plate 25.

294 Clock case, dated 24.8.1787; the spandrels carved by Mr. Williams, two Corinthian capitals and three vases carved by Henry Gibson, turning by Duke Ball; H 8'9" (feet 2½", base 17", trunk 3'6"), dial 13½" (94/84−5).

295 Clock case, dated 27.10.1787; H 7'9" (base 20¼", trunk 3'3½"), dial 13" (94/124−5).

296 Clock case, dated 19.6.1788; mahogany, crossbanded with kingwood and strung with white; H 7'4" (feet 2¼", base 17", trunk 2'10", hood 16" to capitals), dial 13"; made by Christopher Procter (94/322−3).

297 Clock case, dated 22.2.1797; mahogany crossbanded with zebrawood; H 8' (feet 4", base 16¼", trunk 3'6", frieze 2" + 2½", hood 16", top 6" + 1½" + 4¼") × 18½" (base)/14½" (trunk) × 9¾"/7¾" deep, dial 13" (97/1315).

298 Watch case [April 1789] for Mr. Holt, Manchester, no. 9149; mahogany, with frieze of kingwood and inlaid ovals at each end of purplewood; kingwood band round the dial and pediment; spandrels inlaid with yellow fan with blue ends; inlaid fan in pediment marked 'Wht.' (White), base of fan in pediment marked 'Red', base of fan in bottom right-hand corner marked 'Rd' (Red) − it is not a monogram for Richard [Gillow] as stated by Sarah C. Nichols, *Gillow and Company of Lancaster, England: An Eighteenth-Century Business History* (University of Delaware M.A. thesis, 1982, p.159 and plate 22 on p. 160).

299 Bracket clock case, dated [April] 1800, for Mr. Bell, Lancaster; mahogany, crossbanded with mahogany all round the sides, 'birching' mahogany veneer in the front, banded with canary wood, and a double string, black and white, on each side of the band; H 22" × 6" deep, dial 13"; made by Simon Bryham, varnished by Thomas Romney (98/1570).

NOTES ON THE COLOUR PLATES

All the coloured designs are taken from the pattern book in the Westminster City Archives numbered 735/1. Judging from various contemporary pencilled notes (as distinct from much later pencil annotations) this book was shown to Gillows' clients — see e.g. nos. 15 and 16 which recorded details about the customer and his requirements; also a work-table (not illustrated, folio 73) marked 'Have this', which suggests the client's annotation.

These designs are undated. The dating in the notes and captions has been decided by reference to the same design in the Estimate Sketch Books when possible; otherwise it is very approximate.

There are two systems of foliation: the original (written) and a modern, of uncertain date (stamped). Neither is quite complete: both are given here, except where — denotes the absence of foliation.

There is one other feature which is potentially of great significance. Although the majority of these designs evidently relate to the Lancaster manufactory, a small minority apparently do not: nos. 2, 3, 4, 14, 19, 20 in the present selection. In addition, several of the more elaborate pier glasses may belong in this category. If my supposition is correct, the hypothesis must be that these represent the work of the London firm.

1 Two pier or card tables, presumably satinwood and mahogany respectively, about 1785/90 (f.55/53).

2 Two square tables, satinwood and mahogany respectively, about 1785/90 (f.56/54).

3 Pier table, satinwood, inlaid; very close to one made for John Christian in 1788, except for the substitution of an inlaid fan for a shell — see Fig. 11 (f.84/82).

4 Pier table with carved, painted and gilded ornament, and alternative design for the legs. The carved detail is clearly French in inspiration. About 1795 (f.83v/−).

5 Writing-table, satinwood, with secretaire drawer, the top covered with leather. Compare Fig. 41, dated 1794. On view at Hatch Court, Somerset (f.67/65).

6 Writing-table, satinwood, with tambour top. About 1790/95 (f.84v/−).

7 Secretaire with shelves; satinwood, with painted decoration on the cupboard doors. Note the 'tower corners' i.e. angle columns. Compare Fig. 146, dated 1798 (f.−/70).

8 Cabinet with shelves, presumably mahogany and purplewood. Compare Fig. 122, dated 1789. This design was also called 'commode' and 'sheveret' — see note to Fig. 122 (f.71v/−).

9 Cabinet, canarywood with bands of purplewood and tulipwood, strung and double-strung; one made for the London shop, dated 4.12.1795, was the work of Peter Briscoe; H 4' 11¼" × 3' 2½" (top) / 3' 3⅛" (bottom) × 14" — see 97/1218 (f.130v/−).

10 'French' secretaire, satinwood, ebony, and kingwood; cf. Fig. 153 dated 1789 (81/79).

11 Commode chest of drawers, satin-wood and purplewood, with French feet and the characteristic Gillow handles; cf. Fig. 118, dated 1789 (f.81/79).

12 Commode, satinwood and purple-wood, with inlaid and painted orna-ment; supplied to John Christian for Workington Hall in 1788 – see 94/374 (f.87v/opposite 86).

13 Window-cornice with reefed curtain, about 1785/90 (f.125/124).

14 Lady's secretaire, satinwood with painted decoration; a globe beneath. About 1790/95 (f.131/132).

15 Three window-cornices, about 1785/90; no. 2 has a pencilled note 'Tea Room', no. 3 'Mr Stanley' and 'Barré'. Barré is often mentioned in the Waste Books from 1785 on as a colour and it would by very useful if this were it; more probably it means 'this design but in barré colour' (f.126/127).

16 Three window-cornices, about 1785/90. No. 1 has a pencilled note 'Green', no. 2 'Green Ground & Other Colours' (f.127/128).

17 Bed with cornice and hangings; the footposts are a very typical Gillow design (compare those on the Tatton Park bed, Fig. 106, dated 1789) (f.122/121).

18 Couch bed. Cf. Fig. 108, dated 1788 (f.123/122)).

19 Alcove bed, bedsteps, and carpet; apparently after Plate XL at p. 381 in Thomas Sheraton, *The Cabinet-Maker and Upholsterer's Drawing-Book* (Praeger reprint, edited by Charles F. Montgo-mery and Wilfred P. Cole, with an introduction by Lindsay O.J. Boynton, 1970). The engraving is undated, but the *Drawing-Book* was published in 1793. Whether Gillows were using Sheraton or Sheraton plagiarising Gillow will perhaps never be known, but in any event Gillows made the colour-scheme; the carpet was recently woven for Temple Newsam House (f.117/115).

20 Drawing-room window curtains, show-ing alternative cornices &c., and a pier-glass and table. Compare Plate LI at p. 408 of the *Drawing-Book* (as note 19) which is dated 1792; apart from minor differences, mainly in the carpet, it is the same. The colour-scheme was Gillows', of course (f.125/126).

21 Gilt pier-glass frame, about 1790/95. The two vases are in the Wyatt style (f.101v/opposite 99).

22 Gilt pier-glass frame, about 1790/95. The floral sprays are typical features in Gillow designs for pier-glasses and re-lated items; the tripods with rams' heads are again in the Wyatt style (f. –/116).

23 Detail of gilt pier-glass frame and sur-mount; again, the vases are Wyattesque (f.115/112).

24 Two chairs, japanned, about 1785/80 (f.35/34).

25 'English' sofa, about 1790. Bolsters were almost certainly intended (f.49/47).

26 'French' or cabriole sofa, about 1785/90 (f.53/51).

27 Two chairs. (A) shield back with ellip-tical surmount: cf. the chair dated 1789 in Fig. 274. (B) Compare Fig. 281, dated 1788 (f.38/37).

28 Two chairs. (A) Compare 95/663, dated 1790. (B) The lozenge-back was first made in 1792, but this combination with the tablet-back was first recorded in 1797 (f.5/6).

29 Two chairs. (A) Lozenge back (first made in 1792 and continued through-out the '90s); beech, japanned, and varnished. (B) Basket of Flowers back: made in 1796 for clients Tipping and Rigby; see 97/1291 (f.24/24).

30 Two chairs. (A) Square back. This pattern was first recorded in the Waste Books in 1792; it continued in production through the '90s. This version has French-inspired detail and may be dated to the mid or late years of the decade. (B) The Garforth pattern. In 1795 ten chairs with diamond backs, japanned black ground with red were supplied to Peter Garforth of Embsay Hall, Skipton. See 97/1434 (f.39/38).

31 Two chairs. (A) Hall chair, japanned; about 1785/90. (B) Arrowback chair. A set was made in 1795 for Sir William Gerard, of Garswood New Hall. (f.27v/opposite 28).

32 Two chairs. (A) Oval back, japanned; about 1785/80. (B) Square back, about 1790/95 (f.36/35).

INDEX OF PERSONS AND PLACES

INDEX OF WORKMEN

c = carver
cm = cabinet-maker
g = gilder
j = joiner
p = japanner/ornamental painter

Apprentices ('2 lads') F103
Atkinson, G. c.m. F51
Atkinson, George F53
Atkinson, J. p. F106, 107, 256
Atkinson, T. c.m. F.11, 60, 145, 161
Atkinson, Thomas F149
Atkinson, William c.m. F34, 36

Ball, 'Duke' (Marmaduke) turner F79, 86,
    178, 187, 224, 290, 294
Ball, William F70
Bayley c. F95
Baylie, c. F11
Beckett, W. c.m. F50, 144
Beckett, William c.m. F63, 83, 86, 88;
    designer 18
Blackburn, T. c.m. F24, 56
Briscoe, P. c.m. F12, 46
Briscoe, Peter c.m. F119, 120; C9
Brisco, William c.m. F39, 132
Bryan, S. c.m. F168
Bryham, Simon c.m. F299
Burton, James c.m. F15, 34, 85, 152, 153
Burton, James, senior c.m. F155

Cape, John c.m. F167
Charles (? Chailor), W. F110
Clarkson, R. c.m. F97, 101, 146
Clarkson, Robert c.m. F21, 153, 165
Cooper, − F118
Cooper, S. c.m. F10, 50, 91, 92, 101, 121,
    150, 154, 190
Cooper, Samuel c.m. F187, 225
Crookall, − F132
Crowdson, John j. F105, 165

Darwen, Thomas c.m. F98
Dixson, John c.m. F182
Dixon, Christopher c.m. F125
Dobson, Thomas g. F79, 214
Dowbiggin, F. c.m. F17, 38
Dowbiggin, John c., g., inlayer, etc. F6, 48,
    73, 103, 189, 200, 253
Drape, − c.m. F18
Drape, T. c.m. F155

Edmund F124
Edmundson, Robert, junr. c.m. F9
Escolme, T. c.m. F64

Fell, J. F168
Fell, Robert c.m. F30, 41, 127
Ford, John c. & g. F96, 163, 171, 201, 213, 237
Ford, John, Mrs. g. F213
Foster, Joseph F133
Francis, R. chair caner F246

Gaskell, Gatskill, Getskell, William
    c.m. F25, 54, 156, 174
Gibson, Clement c. F179
Gibson, Henry, c. F85, 86, 89, 97, 104, 182,
    187, 225, 227, 229, 253, 267, 273, 287, 293,
    294
Gibson, R. c.m. F16, 62, 70
Gibson, Richard c.m. F145
Greenwood, Robert j. F165

[Harker], Jonathan F198
Harrison, John, chairmaker F256
Hazleton, Hesseldon, Isaac c.m. F115, 139
Hessledon, John c.m. F21, 99
Hodgson, J. c.m. F22, 148
Hodgson, John c.m. F27, 140
Hutton, James p. F17, 228

Jonathan [?Harker] F198
Joseph [?Foster] F124
Joynson, − varnisher F11

Kilner, John c.m., c., also turner F68−9,
    107, 273
King, − F126
Knight, Thomas p. F36, 229

Lambert, Jos. F213
Leeming, Richard F213
Lister, R. c.m. F76
Lister, T. F130
Lupton, C. c.m. F49
Lupton, Charles F188
Lupton, W. c.m. F26
Lupton, William c.m. F29, 57, 72, 124, 133,
    137, 232, 281

INDEX OF FURNITURE

Angles: F10, 15, 92; black, F41, 42, 119; white, F6, 11, 14, 15, 77, 94, 95, 97, 98, 115, 117, 118, 162; black and white F43, 123; purplewood F6, 60

Astragal moulding: F53, 95, 174, 190; edge, F68

Banding (crossbanding, featherbanding, longbanding): F *passim*; with blue veneers F85, 144, 150; with green veneers F60; with purple F5; with black F115, 119, 238, 241; with white F7, 123, 241; in lieu of beads F154

Barré (colour): C.15

Bason stand: Fig. 111

Beds: alcove C19; couch Fig. 108−9, C18; press Fig. 110; bed pillars Fig. 103; bedsteads Fig. 104−7, C17

Beech: F74, 273, 290, 293, C29; simulating bamboo F258

Bookcases: Fig. 156−9; designs for doors Fig. 143; library, Fig. 164−70; and wardrobe Fig. 165; *see also* secretaires and

Bookshelf: Fig. 161; with drawer Fig. 160

Bracket: Fig. 237

Brass: moulding on chair rail F287; *see also* London, items supplied by

Buffets: Fig. 172, 174

Bureau-bookcases: Fig. 138, 140

Bureau and bookshelf: Fig. 22

Bureau writing-table: Fig. 24

Cabinets: Fig. 126−8, 132, C9; with shelves C8

Cabled legs F9, 63, 87, 92, 289; pilasters F174; bed-pillars F107

Canarywood: F46, 97, 140, 299, C9

Candlestand, tripod: Fig. 217

Canterbury: Fig. 239

Cants: F37, 182

Carving: F1, 2, 13, 73, 86, 89, 95, 96, 97, 104, 105, 107, 110, 137, 138, 197, 214, 242, 243, 249, 253, 257, 267, 273, 281, 289, 293, 294; brackets F2, 71; capitals F9, 11, 63, 87, 127, 163, 277, 294; claws F72; drapery F95; feathers F104; husks F13; leaves F11, 179, 289; oakleaves F95, raffle leaves F95; paterae F13, 82 (in solid), F11, 95; ribbon F95; tablets F13, 81, 95, 96; vase F95, 104; wheatears F272

Cedar: F17, 101, 133, 136

Chairs: armchairs Fig. 270, 274, 288, 291; basket of flowers C29B; cabriole Fig. 267, 281; drapery and feather Fig. 273; French Fig. 242; Garforth C30B; gothic Fig. 256, 257; lozenge/diamond Fig. 280, C29A, 30B; reading Fig. 246; shield back C24, 27A; smoking Fig. 244; square back Fig. 284−5, C27B, 30A, 32B; tripod C29A; chairs: arrow back C31B; balloon, old Fig. 264, new Fig. 265; baluster, three upright Fig. 248, 276; 'bamboo' Fig. 258; camel back Fig. 260; Catherine-wheel, new Fig. 269; China Fig. 259; dining Fig. 278, 282−3, 286; fan back Fig. 251, new ditto Fig. 250; hall Fig. 253−5, heart back Fig. 272; oval Fig. 271, C32A; shield back Fig. 261−2, 266, 277, C24; Spanish back Fig. 279; splat − carved Fig. 249, dog-leg Fig. 263, honeysuckle Fig. 268, horizontal Fig. 247, old Fig. 245, pierced Fig 252; tablet top-rail Fig. 286, C28B; Wyatt's Fig. 275

Chest of drawers: Figs. 114−5; commode ditto C11

Cisterns: Figs. 177−9

Clock cases: (longcase) Figs. 294−7; (bracket) Fig. 299

Clothes press: Fig. 131

Commodes: Figs. 18, 117−23, C12; with toilet Fig. 116; chest of drawers C11

Construction *see* angles, astragals, banding, cross/stretching rails, deal veneering on, desk/writing drawers, elevating tops/flaps, fall-fronts, framed back *see* panelled back, mahogany veneered on mahogany, on oak, in solid; oak, veneering on; panels; satinwood, veneering on, in solid; slides; sliding prospect; stringing; triple drawers; writing drawers

Corner cupboard: Fig. 173; for clothes Fig. 175

Cornices: carved and painted Figs. 105, 107; elliptical Fig. 104; new cove Fig. 148; Tuscan Fig. 168

Cornice, window: Figs. 208, 227−31, C13, 15, 16

Cross-rails (stretching-rails): Figs. 28−9, 44−5, 58−9

Curtains, window: C20

Cylinder front: Figs. 47, 49

Damask: F225, 226, 267, 292

Deal: primary F 17, 102, 170−1, 228; secondary F 11, 110, 135, 136, 139, 163, 187; in drawers F132; backs and shelves F144; veneering on, F14, 145

Dentil cornice: F174

Desk and bookcase: Fig. 137; writing, Fig. 141

PART TWO

Indexes to the Gillow Estimate Sketch Books (1784–1800)

   I   Index of Names and Places
  II   Index of Workmen
 III   Index of Furniture

Indexes to the Estimate Sketch Books were compiled by the late G.F. Osborn and their copyright belongs to the Westminster City Archives. The indexes which follow here are edited from Mr. Osborn's by kind permission of Miss M. Swarbrick, Chief Archivist.

INDEX OF NAMES AND PLACES

★indicates that the name is deleted

Atkinson & Dennison (Denison) (Messrs), [of Union Square, Lancaster, merchants], 97/1287

Atkinson & Willock (Messrs.), 97/1287, 1422, 1457

Austin, − 93/390

Austin Friars, London, 96/1140

Auzier, John L., 97/1279

B., W., & Co. (Messrs) (Probably William Brown & Co., of Liverpool, or William Bishop & Co.), 97/1367, 1368(2), 1420, 1443(2); 98/1508

B. & M. (probably Messrs. Burrow & Mason), 97/1338, 1349

Back Lane, Lancaster, 97/1251

Backbarrow, Lancs., 94/39

Backhouse, −, of Manchester, 93/358

Backhouse, John, [of Manchester], 93/253

Backhouse, T[homas, of Beck House], Giggleswick, Yorks., 95/501, 537

Bacon, Thomas, of The Oaks, nr. Wolverhampton, Staffs., 98/1599

Bagot, − 98/1483

Bagot, Lewis see St. Asaph, Lewis Bagot, Bishop of

Bailey (Bayley), − 94/337; 96/1125; 97/1145, 1291

Bailey (Baily, Bayley), − (Mrs.), 93/26, 31, 273

Bailey, [Lawrence], of Blackpool, Lancs., 94/39

Bailey, Samuel, 97/1426

Bailey (Bayly), Samuel (Mrs.), 93/26, 31

Bailey & Taylor (Messrs.), of Liverpool, 97/1447, 1455, 1459

Bain, [William] of Temple Sowerby, Westmorland, 97/1451

Bainbridge, G., 98/1475a

Bains, − 93/547b

Bairstow (Bairstows), − (Miss), [of Preston, Lancs.], 96/1018

Baldwin, − of Wigan, Lancs., attorney, 93/117, 303

Baldwin, [John], attorney, 96/959; 97/1332

Baldwin, John, of Lancaster, attorney, 97/1381

Baldwin, Thomas (Rev.), of Leyland, Lancs., 93/446

Baldwin, W[illiam], of Wigan, Lancs., attorney, 94/212; 95/508

Ball, − 98/1524

Ball, −, of Doubin Lee (Dolphinlee), Lancaster, 94/233

Ball, John, of Bulk, nr. Lancaster, 97/1257

Ball, Robert, of Dolphin Lee (Dolphinlee), [Lancaster], 93/294

Ball, Robert, of Caton, Lancs., 94/186

Ball, William, of Skerton, Lancs., 93/519

Bamber Bridge, Lancs., 97/1309, 1312

Banister, − [(Rev.), of Mowbrick, nr. Kirkham, Lancs.], 95/536

Bank, nr. Manchester & Stockport, Ches., 97/1202, 1206

Bankfield, Lancs., 97/1221

Banks, −, philosopher, 93/5

Banks, − (Mrs.), 93/506

Banks, − 95/lxii (479)

Banks (Bankes), William, of Winstanley, Lancs., 93/14, 22, 34, 95

Bannister, −, of Liverpool, attorney, 98/1539

Barbados, West Indies, 93/280(2)

Barbara (Ship), 93/162, 337, 437, 438

Barber, M., of Lancaster, merchant, 93/547b

Barclay, − 96/1034

see also Norris & Barclay (Messrs)

Bardsea Hall, Lancs., 97/1256

Barker, − (Mrs.), 93/350; 94/238

Barker, − (Mrs), schoolmistress, 93/436, 533

Barnaby, John, [of Brockhampton, Herefordshire], 96/866

Barnard Castle, Durham, 93/208

Barnes, − (Rev.), of Garstang, Lancs., 97/1294, 1296, 1297

Baron, Roger, of Cabin End, [nr. Blackburn, Lancs.], 93/144

Barrington, Shute see Durham, Shute Barrington, Bishop of

Barrock (Barrack) Lodge, Cumberland, 96/1120

Barrow, − 95/673

Barrow, −, limner, 93/36*, 127

Barrow, − (Dr.), 93/18, 23, 146, 162, 182, 231, 285, 374, 411, 425

Barrow, − (Miss), 93/18, 34

Barrow, George, 97/1189

Barrow, J. & Sons (Messrs), 94/xviii(2), 19, 21

Barrow, James, 93/17, 18, 45*, 46, 106, 114, 146, 313, 316, 327, 328, 439, 448, 457, 466, 476, 477, 479, 480, 482, 509, 531, 533; 94/47; 95/584

Barrow, James, attorney, 93/182, 206

Barrow, James (Dr.), 93/466

Barrow, James, of Lancaster, 97/1303

Barrow, Jane (Mrs.), 93/282

Barrow, John & Sons (Messrs.), 95/632, 634, 639, 640, 746

Barrow, Thomas, [of Westby Hall, Lancs.], 93/329, 330(2)

Barrow, William, merchant, 93/232

Barrow, William & Co, 93/301

Barton, − 93/418, 419; 95/lxx (720)

Barton, John, of Manchester, 97/1171

Barwick, − 93/82, 105, 156

Barwick, William, 93/47, 89

Bateman, − (Rev.), 95/507, 514

Bateman, Samuel (Rev.), [of Dodford, nr. Daventry, Northants,], 95/543

Bateson, − 97/1440, 1444

1275, 1277, 1280, 1300, 1303(3), 1357, 1381, 1420; 98/1485, 1536, 1540, 1554, 1570b
see also Back Lane, Castle, Castle Hill, ?Consistory Court, Dolphinlee, Freemasons' Lodge, Friarage, Golgotha Cemetery, High Street, Horse & Farrier, Kings Arms, Leonard Gate, Linen Warehouse, New Inn, New Street, Penny Street, Poorhouse, Quay, Queen Square, Queen Street, Stonewell, Town Hall, White Cross
[Lancaster] Canal [Committee], 96/902
Lancaster (*Ship*), 93/185
Lane, − (Mrs.), 97/1243
Langford, Notts., 98/1546
Langshaw, − 93/184, 381
Langton, − 93/191
Langton, G[eorge] of the Castle, Lancaster, 93/477
Langton, John, of Kirkham, Lancs., 93/95
Langton, [Thomas], of Kirkham, Lancs., 93/541
Langton, William, 96/832, 878, 879, 903, 904, 906
Langton, William, of Kirkham, Lancs., 97/1141
Latham, −, of [Southworth House], Wigan Lane, nr. Wigan, Lancs., 93/295
Lathom House, Lancs., 98/1558
Lauderdale, James Maitland, 8th Earl of, 95/585
Laurel (*Ship*), 95/587(2), 603, 617, 621, 623, 625; 97/1278
Law, − 96/922
Law, [George], of Brathay, Lancs., 93/83, 84
Lawrance, Joseph, of Manchester, 93/527, 529
Lawrence, John, of Manchester, 95/768
Lawrence (Laurence), John, *jnr.*, of Manchester, 94/430, 440; 95/680
Lawson, − 93/114, 122, 180, 218, 274; 94/iv(*416*)
Lawson, − Lady, 98/1505
Lawson, − (Mrs.), 93/473
Lawson, *Sir* John, [of Brough Hall, nr. Richmond, Yorks.], 96/963, 1014
Lawson, John, 93/136, 147, 149, 218, 287, 357, 382, 473; 95/lxix(*582*), 534
Lawson, John (Mrs.), 95/597
Lawson, Robert, 93/86
Leaf, John, of Manchester, 96/832, 1136
Leck, Lancs., 94/418, 436
Lee, − 94/13
Lee, −, of Tooks Court, London, 96/910
Leech, [John], (Rev.), of Blackburn, Lancs., 95/583
Leeds, Yorks., 94/60, 280
Leek, Staffs., 93/481
Lees, − (Mrs.), 93/421
Lees, A. (Mrs.), of Halifax, Yorks., 93/279, 296

Lees, J[ohn], of Halifax, Yorks., 93/138
Lees, Lawrence, 93/421
Lees, [Samuel], of Saville Green, nr. Halifax, Yorks., 93/430
Lees & Harrison, Messrs., 93/380
Leicester, 93/176
Le Fleming, *Sir* Michael, [of Rydal Hall], Westmorland, 97/1402, 1403
Legh, − (Mrs.), [of Heath, Mr. Wakefield, Yorks.], 95/1557
Legh, Henry Cornwall, [of High Legh, nr. Knutsford, Ches.], 95/495
Leicester, [H.A. of Dorfold Hall, nr. Nantwich, Ches.], 95/lxix(*754*)
Leicester, *Sir* John, [of Tabley Hall, nr. Knutsford, Ches.], 95/668
Leicester, 93/176; 97/1211, 1384
Leigh, − (Miss), 97/1416
Leigh, − (Miss), of Whitley, [Wigan], Lancs., 96/1084
Leigh, − (Mrs.), 93/291
Leigh, − (Mrs.), of Leigh Place, nr. Wigan, Lancs., 93/203, 204, 223, 237, 293, 548; 94/226, 396, 410; 95/xx(*471*), lix(*730*), 467, 505
Leigh, − (Mrs.), [of Whitley], Wigan, Lancs., 96/838, 1032(2), 1040, 1069
Leigh (Lee), T., 94/xxxviii(*294*), lvii(*288*), 280
Leigh, Thomas, 94/292
Leigh Place, Lancs., 93/203, 223, 237, 293; 94/226
Leighton, ?Lancs., 93/302
Leighton Hall, Lancs., 97/1392, 1401
Leo, − 97/cxv(*1386*); 96/1131
Leo, Daniel, of Llanerch Park, nr. St. Asaph, Denbigh, 96/1017, 1021, 1119, 1121, 1135; 97/1185
Leonard, George, 93/427
Leonard Gate, Lancaster, 93/337★
Leonardson, Allan, 93/186
Lethbridge, − 95/lxx(*493*)
Lethbridge, John, [of Sandhill Park, nr. Taunton, Somerset], 94/li(*296*); 96/993, 998
Lewtas, [Matthew], of Poulton, Lancs., 93/390
Leyland, Lancs., 93/446; 97/1176
Lind, [G., of Burton in Kendal, Westmorland], 94/41
Lindow, − 93/184, 255, 288
Lindow, − (Mrs.), 93/355, 370, 404, 458, 469, 487, 499, 530, 534, 544, 557; 95/482, 488, 559, 588
Lindow, H.L., of Grassyard Hall, Lancs., 98/1494
Lindow, William, 93/45(2), 124, 205
Linen warehouse, Lancaster, 97/1541
Lister, − 94/253; 95/616, 715, 748, 785; 96/845, 968, 998, 1031
Lister, − (Mrs.), 93/272
Lister, [Thomas], of Gisburn Park, Yorks.,

96/869, 887

Marriott, (Marriot), William, [of Manchester], 98/1475a,b, 1480, 1493

Marsden, −, of Farfield, Yorks., 93/480

Marsden, John, [of Hornby, Lancs.], 97/ci(*1194*), cxi(*1194*); 95/598

Marsden, John, of Wennington, Lancs., 93/104; 96/lxxxix(*1117*)

Marshall, −, [of Workington, Cumberland], 97/1275

Marshfield, Yorks., 93/196

Martin, T., 98/1543

Martin, Thomas, 98/1472, 1483, 1484

Martinique, West Indies, 97/1431

Marton, − (Dr.), 93/111, 120, 371

Marton, − (Mrs.), 96/903, 924

Marton, − (Rev.), 93/291

Mashiter, − 98/1523, 1528, 1529(3)
    see also Housman, Mashiter & Co. (Messrs.)

Mason, − 97/1413; 98/1521, 1527
    see also Burrow & Mason (Messrs.)

Mason, − (Miss), of Eshton, Yorks., 96/1028

Mason, J., 93/415, 416, 424, 456

Mason, Jackson, [of Lancaster, attorney], 95/565, 620

Mason, James, 93/434, 513; 94/164−5

Mason, Miles (Myles), [of Sedbergh, Yorks.], 93/274; 95/482

Mate of the Ship Caton, 93/487

Mather, Samuel, 93/248

Matthews, − 98/1590

Matthews, W., 98/1475b

Matthews, William, of Liverpool, 98/1598

Maude, − (Miss), of Kendal, Westmorland, 97/1148

Maude, − (Mrs.), of Kendal, Westmorland, 98/1482

Maude, Joseph, of Kendal, Westmorland, 93/246; 95/658

Maudsley, − 93/69

Maudsley, Stephen, [of Clapham-cum-Newby, Yorks.], 93/360

Maxwell, − 97/1423, 1424

Maxwell, James [of Kirkconnel, nr. Dumfries, Kirkcudbright], 96/913

Meadowcraft, − (Mrs.), of Oldham Street, Manchester, 97/1287

Meriden, Warw., 94/452

Metcalf, [Thomas], of Keighley, Yorks., 97/1383

Middle Temple, London, 95/529

Middleton, Dorothy (Miss), 93/235

Middleton, William, of Stockeld, nr. Wetherby Yorks., 93/138, 145

Middlewich, Ches., 98/1482

Miles (Myles), Sarah (Mrs.), of [Douglas], Isle of Man, 98/1462

Milford, Richard Philipps, Baron, 96/944★

Millars, Thomas, of Lancaster, 97/1262

Miller, − (Miss), 97/1169

Mill Hill, Blackburn, Lancs., 93/445, 470

Mills, Thomas, of Leek [& Barlaston,]. Staffs., 93/416, 481

Milne, [Richard, of Rochdale, Lancs., attorney], 96/1019

Milne, Richard (Mrs.), of Rochdale, Lancs., 97/1263

Milner, *Sir* William, of Nun Appleton, Yorks., 95/518, 560

Milnthorpe, Westmorland, 94/364

Mingay (Mingey), − 95/751, 756; 96/1049

Molloy, − (Capt.), 97/1178, 1187, 1188

Molly (*Ship*), 93/171

Montagu, George Samuel Browne, 8th Viscount, 96/937

Moon, −, nr. Garstang, Lancs., 93/299

Moore, − 97/1359
    see also Benson & Moore (Messrs.)

Moore (Moor), − (Major), [of Grimeshill, Westmorland], 93/121, 262, 294★

Moore, James, 93/141

Moreland, − 93/31

Morland, − 93/257(2), 409, 450

Morland, − (Mrs.), 93/268

Morland, − (Mrs.), of [Capplethwaite Court], Kendal, Westmorland, 93/334

Morland, John, of Capplethwaite, Westmorland, 93/244, 258, 410, 426, 515

Morville Hall, Salop., 95/614

Mostyn, John M., of Segroit, nr. Denbigh, 97/1191

Mountain, John, of Chipping, Lancs., 94/41

Much Woolton, Lancs., 93/207

Muncaster, John Pennington, 1st Baron, [of Muncaster House, nr. Ravenglass, Cumberland], 93/xii(*128*), 70, 116, 151

Murray, [James, of York], 96/1022

Myddelton, − (Miss), of Denbigh, N. Wales, 93/166, 169, 170

Myers, − (Mrs.), 93/221

Nantwich, Ches., 96/1138

Napier, − (Capt.), The Hon., [of Ulverston, Lancs.], 96/1096

Naylor, − 95/507, 763;

Naylor, [William, of Liverpool], 96/964

Nelson, − (Mrs.), [of Fairhurst, nr. Wigan, Lancs.], 96/884

Nerquis, Flint., 95/793

Netherby, Cumberland, 95/755

Netherhall, Cumberland, 97/1197

Netting, − 95/lix(*582*)

New Inn, Lancaster, 96/833, 891; 98/1466

New Street, Lancaster, 93/102, 461, 517; 95/626; 97/1460

Newbottle, Co. Durham, 95/651, 652

Newcastle-upon-Tyne, Northumberland *see* Clavering Place, Pilgrim Street

Newdigate, *Sir* Roger, [of Arbury Hall, nr.

INDEX OF WORKMEN

★ indicates that two name is deleted. ★★ page missing — index entry only.

Allen drawings more record 66-72
"Shop lists 1767-98
17 connect on Shorter
71 connect on importance Allen
sketchbook.
also bibliography

INDEX OF FURNITURE

This index excludes references without sketches: for these, consult the typescript indexes at the Westminster City Archives Centre.